A Gathering of Angels

Seeking Healing
after an Infant's Death

Compiled and Edited by
Victoria Leland, RN

In Collaboration with Five Grieving Mothers:
Audra Fox-Murphy, Heather Gray, Linda Bailey,
Sahnewaz (Tania) Hossain, and Allison Guild

acta
PUBLICATIONS

A GATHERING OF ANGELS
Seeking Healing after an Infant's Death
Compiled and Edited by Victoria Leland, RN
In Collaboration with Five Grieving Mothers: Audra Fox-Murphy, Heather Gray,
Linda Bailey, Sahnewaz (Tania) Hossain, and Allison Guild

Edited by Andrew Yankech
Cover design by Tom A. Wright
Text design and typesetting by Patricia A. Lynch

Scripture quotes are from the *New Revised Standard Version of the Bible*, copyright © 1989 by the Division of Christian Education of the National Council of the Churches of Christ in the USA. All rights reserved. Used with permission.

Published by ACTA Publications, 4848 N. Clark Street, Chicago, IL 60640, (800) 397-2282, www.actapublications.com

Library of Congress Number: 2010927569
ISBN: 978-0-87946-427-1

Printed in The United States by Evangel Press
Year 16 15 14 13 12 11 10
Printing 10 09 08 07 06 05 04 03 02 First Edition

Contents

We lovingly dedicate this book
to the memory of our angel babies:

Gabriel Fox
Connor Gray
Madison Bailey
Lanika Hossain
Brennen Guild

*If our love could have saved you,
you would have all lived forever.*

Introduction

*"A gathering of angels
can enlighten the whole world."
— Anonymous*

*D*id your baby die, leaving you to bear a grief that is so beyond definition that everything in your life has instantly changed and must now be redefined? Has your spark for life been extinguished, your hope for the future vanquished, and your understanding of life shattered? Do you feel like a shell of your former self? Have you searched for a salve for your terrible hurt—in family, friends, prayer, support groups, church, books, drugs, alcohol, etc.—and found help in some measure, but still you walk away hurting, disappointed, and feeling beyond help? If so, I want you to know first that I am truly very sorry for your loss. I can't imagine the depth of the pain you must bear. But, I also want you to know you are not alone in your terrible grief. You are in need of good and special souls. You are in need of angels. Have you found any yet?

I have.

Or is there a special loved one in your life who is grieving the loss of a baby? Do you want to help but don't know how? Are you trying to understand what your loved one must be thinking or feeling? Do you feel inadequate and unable to say or do anything that can help? You also are in need of angels. Have you found any yet?

I have.

Although we live in a medically advanced society, tens of thousands of babies are torn away from life too soon by miscarriage, stillbirth, prematurity, birth defects, SIDs, disease, and accidents. A multitude of young mothers and fathers are left behind to suffer gaping wounds caused by the tragic loss of their babies. These parents live on with an insatiable hunger for clarity as they process what has happened, all the while searching for words of true understanding and for effective solace as they mourn their beloved children. But when they search for help, all too often they find a society that largely underestimates the deepness of their loss. Our society is inclined to dismiss these early deaths and tries to minimize parents' grief, wrongly assuming that because the child lived so short a time, the grief associated with their loss cannot be that great. It is assumed recovery will be brief and life should quickly return to normal. Nothing could be further from the truth. You know this. Good and special souls ("angels") know this. Have you found any angels yet?

I have.

The term "angel" is used quite loosely today, conjuring many different interpretations. For the purposes of this book I am defining an angel in two different ways:

(1) first, as that lovely soul who lived and died in your midst, touched you to your very core, and although gone from you now, continues to leave a legacy of love deep in your heart. It is very evident to all involved that God deemed a very special purpose for their life;

(2) second, as that lovely soul who appears in your life, sometimes briefly, sometimes with longevity, who is compassionately available to you in your grief—someone who doesn't run from it, ignore it, minimize it, or try to fix it. This good and special soul "gets it." No matter how unexplainable and confounding your grief, he or she chooses to walk alongside you in your journey.

Have you found any such angels yet?

I have. I am Victoria Leland, RN (known as "Vicky" to my friends), and I feel compelled to share a unique experience that has permeated the many layers of who I am. It has affected my life as a nurse, photographer, March of Dimes volunteer, writer, Christian, and friend.

Beginning in the summer of 2006 and over the following nine months, a remarkable group of individuals assembled around me. I was working as a bedside nurse in a busy Neonatal Intensive Care Unit (NICU) in Plano, Texas, when five precious babies in my unit died. After nearly twenty years of NICU nursing, I had come to know many wonderful parents and, yes, I had seen many babies die. There was something inexplicably unique, however, in how these five families touched me. Other families came and went and other babies died in my NICU during that time (2006 was an unusually tough year in my NICU). But a spark of true connection ignited when I encountered these five families, especially the mothers.

First there was Audra, a twenty-three-year-old, newly married young woman with so many grand plans for a lovely life with her new husband and first baby. She was a bank teller and her husband was in the army, recently back from a tour of duty in Iraq. Despite all the best medical care they received, their son Gabriel arrived when Audra was only six months into her pregnancy. He did relatively well at first in the NICU, and as he grew it looked as if he'd go home soon. But tragedy struck—part of his intestines suddenly died, leaving him deathly ill. Gabriel lived only sixty-two days, and left his young parents completely devastated.

Shortly after Gabriel died, I met Heather. Heather was a professional engineer who had spent her first ten years out of college building a very successful career and marriage. She and her husband Cole excitedly anticipated the birth of their first child, but he came extremely early into Heather's pregnancy. Connor was born at twenty-four weeks gestation, which is just past the point in a pregnancy when some babies can be saved. Connor struggled from the onset of his brief life, his lungs and immune system simply too immature to sustain him. He died at twenty days of age, leaving his adoring parents completely crushed.

While I was caring for Connor, I also met Linda. Linda was an accountant and mother of twin girls born at twenty-four weeks gestation. Madison died at only two days of age. Kaitlyn, however, survived her premature beginnings after a very lengthy stay in the NICU. Linda and her husband Brendan grieved the loss of one child, while, with their other child, they endured all the stresses and strains that go with a four-month NICU stay. While Linda and Brendan were ecstatic over Kaitlyn's survival, this in no way lessened their grief over the loss of their beloved Madison. Their hopes of raising both twin daughters were shattered, and they were left overwhelmed with grief at Madison's death.

A few months later I met Tania, a native of Bangladesh who had come to the United States as a teenager ten years earlier. She and her husband Sunny were the proud parents of two daughters and Lanika, who arrived twenty-seven weeks into Tania's pregnancy. Lanika did very well in the NICU initially, but at six weeks of age she caught a terrible infection that her frail little body could not surmount. When she died, her parents and sisters were completely overcome with grief. So many of their hopes and dreams for their family died along with Lanika.

And a few months later, I came to know Allison, a special education teacher who had excitedly awaited her first child. But complications set in half-way through her pregnancy, and she endured eight weeks of strict bed rest before Brennen arrived at twenty-eight weeks gestation. She and her husband Brian prayed and hoped for his survival, but he lived for only nine days. They walked away from the NICU empty-handed and brokenhearted.

After these five babies died, I watched with great sadness as their remarkable young mothers plunged into the dark abyss of overwhelming grief, and I could not help but befriend them all. They each moved me, inspired me, touched me—in their motherhood and in their grief—and I felt strongly drawn to each of them. Until that point, I had occasionally befriended parents in crisis in the months and years after their discharge from the NICU. But these five babies and their mothers were somehow very different. Quite simply, I can explain it no other way than that they must have been angels to me. Almost from the moment we first met, they all instantaneously entered a very special place in my heart in ways I find difficult to articulate. I still marvel at this rare coming together of hearts. And I still marvel at them—good and special souls, each and every one.

It is a cold, sad fact that every day in this frenzied rhythm of our twenty-first century existence, babies die. While the busy world might not much have noticed these particular five babies' lives, I did. I remember them. They were angels who gathered in my midst.

And a gathering of angels can enlighten the whole world.

I want to tell you how they enlightened me.

The Angels Set to Work

$\mathcal{J}$ first gathered these five grieving women together shortly after Brennen's death, inviting them each to join me in a volunteer project I was working on for the March of Dimes called "The Path of Hope." They were eager to be involved in something that advanced the cause of healthy babies, and each of them felt the need to do something meaningful that honored the memories of their babies. It took literally no time for Audra, Heather, Linda, Tania, and Allison to form a very special bond and to connect with one another through their grief and compassion. Friendships were easily forged by their common desire to make something good come from the terrible tragedy that had befallen them.

Once that initial March of Dimes project was completed, this group of ladies did not want to stop meeting. They needed one another! They had each experienced feelings of terrible isolation in their grief and learned that our society rarely knows how to help a grieving parent. The group decided to meet regularly, openly share their grief journeys, and then combine their accumulated thoughts into a book. This book would be the legacy of Gabriel, Connor, Madison, Lanika, and Brennen, five angel babies who came and went much too quickly from our lives, but left a deep, lasting impact on us all. We affectionately came to call ourselves the "Good Grief Group," and we set ourselves in earnest to this good task.

The Role of the Fathers
I want to state that the fathers involved here were a large influence in this endeavor. A couple's grief in the aftermath of the death of a baby is most definitely a journey of two. After the death of their babies, Erik, Cole, Brendan, Sunny, and Brian all grieved profoundly. Because of work and other responsibilities, these men were not as available to me as were their wives. When the Good Grief Group focused on this book, these men all supported our efforts. Some of the fathers cared for the children at home after their long work days, enabling their wives to participate in our Good Grief Group gatherings. As the mothers wrote, they often discussed thoughts with their husbands and incorporated a dad's perspective whenever possible. The love of these fathers left a deep impression in many of the words

you'll read, and their presence is most assuredly felt between the lines of this book.

First Steps

The first goal I set for the Good Grief Group was to draft a list of what they thought were the fifteen hardest "things" about grieving. At our first book writing gathering, we sat around my dining room table and brainstormed ideas: the mothers telling me everything that was so difficult for them in their grief journey, and me frantically trying to write all their thoughts on a large tablet of paper I'd put up on an easel. In an hour, we filled up more than eight large sheets of paper identifying what they struggled with in their grief.

I worked to condense their eight pages of ideas into fifteen "themes" that would be a good summation of what is most difficult in a parent's grief journey, as identified by these five women. Try as I may, I could not get the long list they voiced to me down to that small a number. I was learning that grief pervades everything, and the difficulties that result are endless. I was able to eventually condense their list to twenty-one broad themes, which they agreed represented their most difficult challenges with grief.

I was clear from the onset with these five grieving mothers that I was not professionally trained as a grief counselor; I would not have the answers to their many probing questions. This did not seem to matter to them. They knew I was hungry to learn, and they were very willing to share their experiences with me. I desired to be a part of this group in order to listen and learn, not advise. I wanted them to teach me about grief so that I could understand it better, be more helpful to them, and eventually assist future grieving parents more effectively.

And so, what follows is what our Good Grief Group discussed and identified as our grief themes. These discussions took place over a time frame of about two years. If you read chronologically from the first to the last theme, you will see a progression of these women's grief. The initial eleven themes were written in the first year after their babies died, when their grief was extremely raw and intense. These themes primarily focus on expressing how their grief felt. The next eleven themes were written in their second year of grief, and in them I believe the grieving mothers began to show an acquired wisdom in their journeys toward peace.

How might the following pages be helpful to you? It is our hope that, if you are a parent who has lost a baby, they will:

- Help you clarify your thoughts and understanding about your grief.
- Give words to your grief experience in ways you may not have found yet on your own.
- Bring you some reassurance that you are not strange or going crazy because of the way you think and act after the death of your baby.
- Help you realize you are not alone—we hope to lessen your feelings of isolation as you identify with others.
- Provide you comfort in knowing these six women care and want to help any parent experiencing intense grief.
- Offer you suggestions that may help you in your grief journey.
- Bring you hope that happiness is possible in your life again.

If you are the loving friend or family member of someone journeying through the terrible grief of losing a baby, we hope the following pages will:

- Provide you better insight into this unique type of grief.
- Offer you suggestions that will make you more comfortable as you try to assist your grieving loved one.
- Enable you to effectively help someone you care very much about through their grief.

How to Read This Book

$\mathcal{W}$e realize people who pick up this book will come to it with a wide variety of needs. It may not be helpful for everyone to read what we have written in the typical way one reads a book: from start to finish. You may find yourself skipping around rereading certain sections, and *that is okay*. Grief does not follow a straight line, so neither may your experience with this book. We recommend you read in whatever order helps you most. We purposefully placed our chapter about hope at the beginning of our book (even though it was the last thing we wrote) because we recognize the universal need to seek out hope.

Part I

As stated earlier, the first eleven themes are an examination of how early, profound grief feels. They were written only weeks and months after these mothers lost their babies—understandably, you will see deep anger, pain, and questioning in their writings. If you: (1) are new to grief and looking to put words to your own grief feelings, or (2) believe no one else in the world feels and thinks like you do now, or (3) are confused at your angry and lonely feelings, then these chapters can offer you something with which to identify. They are in no way meant to be a prescription for how you should feel as you grieve. Rather, they are an honest sharing of how these particular five women felt as they grieved. Some of it you will identify with, some of it you will not. This will be proof to you that everyone's grief is unique and flows along varying paths and at different paces.

If you want to understand a loved one who is in the throes of deep grief after the loss of a baby, these first eleven chapters will help you more clearly understand what a grieving parent might be experiencing. Some of it will not seem logical to you, because grief is intensely emotional and often defies logic. If you find yourself thinking, "They shouldn't feel that way," then you are missing the point. The fact of the matter is that these five grievers felt these things, whether they're logical or not, and whether you think they should feel these things or not. Read these initial chapters wanting to learn what their experience was, instead of trying to decide for them what their experience should have been. We hope these initial chapters, by giving you a greater understanding of a grief experience, will empower you to more effectively understand and help your loved ones through their grief journey.

Part II

The final eleven themes presented in our book begin to examine the wisdom born of a grief experience. They were written when these women's grief had progressed beyond the intense first year of their journey. In these final nine chapters, Audra, Heather, Linda, Tania, and Allison still hurt deeply and yearn for their babies, but they are beginning to find their way toward peace. They are living lives full of love, feeling joy again, and finding ways to make good come from bad. If you yearn to gain wisdom born from the experience of your loss, these chapters will give you food for thought. And if you are looking for a list of ways to try to cope with your grief (written by persons speaking from experience), theme number twenty-two is for you.

We attempted to make our book helpful not only for one individual at a time, but for a group gathering as well. We've structured it in such a way that a group could easily follow our example. The Good Grief Group would be honored if counselors, grief support groups, or church grief ministries came to use *A Gathering of Angels* as a guide for supporting grieving parents. We found what we did together to be highly effective in journeying through grief. We have now attempted to make it easy for someone else to recreate our footsteps.

We readily acknowledge that we do not have the golden answers to surviving the loss of a baby. No one does. Audra, Heather, Linda, Tania, and Allison are five grieving mothers who are in better places now than when their babies died. Today they have hope, feel joy, and laugh, but they still intensely miss their babies. They continue, as they will throughout their lives, journeying toward peace. Their way will not exactly be your way. What we offer to you here is what we can: a gathering of angels, who by honestly sharing their experience hope to enlighten the world about the journey toward understanding and healing in the aftermath of an infant's death.

We realize people who read this book may come to it with very heavy hearts that are not ready to hear the sad stories of others. Therefore, we placed our lengthier introduction to the Good Grief Group at the back of the book. If, as you read and come to know the authors through their writings, you become curious and want to know more about them, it is there for you in the chapter called "The Gathering." You can go to it whenever your heart is ready—maybe now, maybe much later, maybe not at all. We've left it up to you to decide when is right for you.

Our Message of Hope

*T*he Good Grief Group was more than two years into our grief journey when we wrapped up our efforts to write this book. It was not hard for me to see that Audra, Heather, Linda, Tania, and Allison all were still hurting inside. They were not done with their grief. Their babies may have died, but their motherhood did not. Their love for their babies will go on forever, and their heartache will never completely go away. On the other hand, I could see these women were living very full lives brimming with love and purpose. I knew they all laughed and felt joy again, and were proceeding now with a great mission in life. I often observed the five of them with their families, at work, and in the community bringing hope to others. They have touched so many people in so many positive ways these past two years, and they fully intend to keep doing so.

As we put the finishing touches on our book, I felt it time to ask if they had a final message of hope for other grieving parents. I posed one last set of questions to them: "If you were to meet a mother or father on the street tomorrow who just lost and buried their baby, what would you say to them? What words would you share that could bring a sense of solace to them? What would your advice be to them as they begin to face the difficult road ahead?"

What follows is their response. These are not empty words. They are spoken with honesty and great conviction by five beautiful women who were plunged into profound grief when their babies died two years ago. They have made great strides in their grief journey, and continue in the direction of finding their peace. This is Audra, Heather, Linda, Tania, and Allison's message of hope to you:

You are going to survive this.

Your world is simply going to stop for a while. It needs to. Don't feel left behind. And don't try to keep up. Let it go, and do what you need to do for yourself and your family right now.

You will be okay and happy again.

As hard as it may be to believe, you will laugh again, and eventually not feel guilty about it.

You will learn (slowly at first) to hope and trust again. When you do this, life will feel manageable once more to you.

The death of your baby will have its greatest impact on you. Because you were that child's parent, no one else is going to feel, think, or react quite like you will. Others will also experience grief, but theirs will be different from yours and will progress at a different pace. This is not a bad thing, it's just the way it is, and it can be very frustrating until you realize this truth.

Some of your friends and family will rise up beautifully to support you. Hold on to them. They will be real treasures to you. Other family and friends will not. Supporting people through grief is not something everyone knows how to do or can do. For those you expected would support you and didn't or couldn't, forgive and move on. Holding a grudge against them will serve no purpose.

Your baby made a difference in this world, no matter how long or short his or her life.

God will not leave you abandoned in your grief. Lean on your faith.

Grief will make you rethink many things in your life. You will go through a process of "falling in love all over again"—with your husband or wife, with your children, with your friends, with family members. They all will take on a new significance to you.

You will be able to put the pieces of your heart back together. A piece of it may be missing, but it can mend.

All life is a gift from God. Our children are gifts given to us, and are only ours for a while. They (and we) eventually go back to God.

It is not your fault your baby died.

Purpose in suffering becomes apparent with searching and time— search for the purpose of your suffering.

In your grief, you will come to a point where you have to choose a bitter or a better life. It's up to you. The choice of better is the harder route. Don't give in to the bitterness, which is so easy to do. You can waste your sorrow, or use it for the betterment of yourself and others.

It's your choice.

Drugs and alcohol are not the answer. Don't look for relief from your grief in them. You won't find it there.

Grief will demand your energy and attention. It won't go away if you try to ignore it, hide it, fake it. You must deal with it, no matter how painful or exhausting it is to do so.

You have every right to say, "This sucks," because it does. You have the right to say, "It sucks that this happened to my baby. It sucks that this happened to me." But don't get stuck in that thought for too long. Think it. Feel it. Say it. Scream it. But then move on.

Don't lose sight of the many blessings in your life, for surely there are many. Count your blessings and appreciate them.

Don't grieve alone. Sharing grief can divide it.

Journaling is extremely helpful as it clarifies your thoughts and emotions. It's easier to have a list of topics (such as our themes) to journal about instead of opening a blank journal and not knowing where to begin.

Find a confidant who lets you talk, cry, and question. Find someone who won't try to fix you, advise you, make you stop crying, or even really try to console you, but rather who just lets you express whatever you need to express. Find a confidant who won't judge you as you go through this, and who is willing to give you all the time you need.

Don't be afraid to seek professional counseling.

Use this book as a tool.

Know you are really much stronger than you might ever think possible.

Don't waste your time sweating the small stuff—you of all people know life is too short for that.

Think with purpose. Act with mission.

You are going to survive this.

The Wisdom of Angels

PART I

Grief Defined

Knowing we were going to explore in-depth the experience of their grief, I thought it best if our group effort started by defining the term "grief" itself. I asked these five women, whose grief was still raw and new, "How would you define your grief?" (Allison was two months into her grief, and the others were five-to-eight months into theirs.) Even though they each knew grief intimately, it was not easy for them to define what they were experiencing. How exactly do you define something that defies and permeates everything? I believe they found a way.

Linda Grief is a bottomless void that can never be filled. This void leaves such an emptiness and loneliness within you that, although you may be existing, you're not really living. You may be going through the motions just as you did before, but it's with altogether different feelings. At first, some days it takes all your energy to just exist, but as time goes on, you rediscover the strength to actually live.

Allison I don't think grief can have a definition, because there aren't adequate words to describe it. It's not an emotion; it's a way of life. I don't just wake up in the morning feeling grief; I live it every day. I've heard and like the analogy of the leg amputee—having a vital part of you severed forever, going through many stages of recovery and therapy to learn to walk without it, experiencing intense pain, but eventually beginning to walk again. With grief, the beginning steps are extremely clumsy, and there are falls, frustrations, and disappointments. So much energy is spent on just finding balance so that you don't fall into some deep, bottomless pit. Eventually you can take small steps, which slowly become walking again. Even so, one will never have the same stride they once did, nor even the same ease and confidence in walking they once had. Grief knocked my feet completely out from under me. I am walking again. But my gait will never be the same.

Audra Grief comes uninvited, envelopes your life, and is all-consuming. It's inescapable, although in time we learn to cope with it and compensate. It ebbs and flows, some days fading, and some days, unprovoked and unannounced, it is there, painful as ever. There is reprieve and armor for the struggle—in our inner strength, our faith, and in our experiences of love.

Heather Grief is almost indescribable. Many people have said to me, "I can't imagine how you must feel." I have learned, for the most part, they really can't. Nor would I want them to—I wouldn't wish this on anyone. Immediately after Connor's death, the grief in me was overwhelming: It was the one emotion that overruled all others. I lived my daily life in total grief, going through the motions of daily life, but feeling nothing but total, overwhelming grief. Now, others outside my grief want me to stop it, and stop it quickly, because it is uncomfortable for them. But I love Connor so much it literally hurts. He is worth every bit of the time and energy it is taking me to grieve his death. My grief is indescribable, but the words I would use in some attempt at defining it would be: okay, natural, life-altering, never gotten over, all-encompassing. Grief defines me now more than I can ever define it.

Tania Grief is the very natural, human process for healing emotional injury. It is individual. When I lost my lovely daughter, I lost my breath. Like my other two daughters, she was everything to me. When she died, I felt there was no way I could breathe without her, live without her. When grief knocked on my door, I could not recognize what life was anymore. Grief affected me completely—emotionally, physically, and mentally. I felt extreme, intense sadness, fear, anxiety, anger, depression, loneliness, confusion, helplessness, isolation, and guilt. I lost, for a while, the ability to feel love or to give love, thinking all the while I was going crazy. But I know I am not going crazy. I just know life differently now. Good things, happy things, are slowly returning to my daily life. I love being a mother to my two daughters at home. They have and always will be great joys to me. But my lovely daughter Lanika died. She lay dead next to me in a box, and I had to put her in the ground and say a final goodbye to her. I am not done with my grieving process. Grief is natural. Grief is individual. And I am not done.

GRIEF DEFINED

REFLECTIONS

FOR THE GRIEVING PARENT:
How would you define your grief?

FOR THE FAMILY AND FRIENDS OF A GRIEVING PARENT:
What have you learned about grief from these definitions? Is your definition of grief different from your loved one's definition?

Vicky I am an outsider looking in on these women's grief. I have never experienced what they are experiencing. I have not lost a baby. My closest experience to what they are living was when my eighty-four-year-old grandmother, whom I loved and cherished very much, died. My grief over her passing was extremely intense, but it was different from what I see Audra, Heather, Linda, Tania, and Allison experiencing. My grandmother lived a long life, blessing me for over forty years, and although I greatly mourn her absence, my beloved grandmother's death followed a "proper order" in the cycle of life. It is significant that I was given ample time to say goodbye to her. Sometimes I still cry when I recall my lovely memories of her. Yet I know that what Audra, Linda, Heather, Tania and Allison are experiencing is much deeper and more intense than anything I've felt in the wake of my grandmother's death. I have no right to say to these five women, "I know how you feel," because I don't. Their grief over their babies and my grief over my grandmother are two very different types of grief. They can hardly be compared. When I lost my grandmother, I lost a part of my past. When these women lost their babies, they lost a significant part of their future. The grief after the loss of a baby is very distinctive, with its own considerations, challenges, and depths, and it must be acknowledged as such. I want to try to better understand this very unique type of grief, to try to fathom it, so that I can ultimately know how to better help Audra, Heather, Linda, Tania, Allison, and other grieving parents. And so, I will not begin an attempt at defining this type of grief. Although I have dealt with many parents whose babies have died, I confess my ignorance. I have never really listened to their pain. I will open my heart and listen to these five courageous young women, for I know they have much to teach me.

THEME 2

Feeling Robbed

Tania It feels like I have been robbed all my life. When I was in sixth grade, my dad passed away. I lost my first pregnancy at six weeks. My mom passed away in 2004. I loved my parents very much. When my mom passed away, I felt as though I lost the shade over my head. When she left, she took my laughter with her. But I eventually found my way to happiness again: I had my husband, my two beautiful daughters, and I felt the joy of a third, beloved child growing inside of me. I had plenty to smile about again in my life. But then the thief returned. My Lanika stayed for only a little time. So many of the people in my life, whom I love so much, stay too little a time with me. This thief, how much will it take from me in my life? How much do I have to cry? It's not material things I've been robbed of: It is feelings, love, and dreams. There is no one I can blame for robbing me, no matter how much I may want to. I can't strike out and I can't yell at this thief like I want to. What I have learned is this: Our loved ones live among us, and they die among us. We love them while they are with us, and we miss them terribly when they are gone. Death is as much a part of life as living is. I am so grateful that my husband and two other daughters have remained with me. I just wish my other loved ones stayed with me a while longer—that I wasn't robbed of the chance to love them like I wanted to.

Allison Until Brennen, I had never actually lost anything of great value. I have, however, moved several times in my life, and I know the eeriness of a home when all your possessions have been taken out, and all you are left with are the blank walls, empty rooms, and all the memories of how it used to look and the comfort that it once brought. Through my moving experiences, I can try to imagine the kick in the chest or slap on the face that would come from returning home one day to find out you'd been robbed of all your possessions. You'd know what should be where and how things should look and feel, only to find blank walls, empty rooms, and the memories of what once was. That is how my life feels right now…this is how my home feels without Brennen. He should be here. I've been robbed of the most precious, most desired thing imaginable. I know in my heart and mind how things should be, but all that I am left with is a vacant crib, empty arms, silent rooms, and too few memories. I was robbed of so many things: I was robbed of a full-term, healthy pregnancy. I did not get to watch in delight and wonder over nine months as my body grew with life. I was robbed of my motherhood and the opportunities to counsel my firstborn son, marvel at the innocence of his childhood, and watch him grow into a man. My future, as I planned it, was taken from me. I was robbed of my own innocence. Taken from me was the ability to experience a good time, a family celebration, or a holiday without that silent wish in my heart that Brennen was with us to join in the goodness of it all. I was robbed of my son, and nothing in this lifetime can ever replace him. Most women wait for nine months to be with their child. I will now have to wait my entire life.

Linda I have been robbed of so many things:

(1) ***My old life, my old self:*** My old life had concerns such as stress over work and other minor worries I now know really didn't matter. My new life is filled with such things as grief sup-

port groups, regular visits to the cemetery, and a deep sadness for a child I loved and now miss desperately. I never knew how simple my old life was.

(2) *My feelings of invincibility:* I never thought anything like this could ever happen to me. I live a good life, try to do what's right, and try to help others. If you had told me a few years ago that I'd be burying my child, I would never have believed you, because I knew that I would do everything I was supposed to do. But I have learned it doesn't work that way in real life. I have learned, no matter what I do, that I am vulnerable, and those whom I love are also vulnerable.

(3) *Fairy tale endings:* Most everyone I know has wonderful stories of how their children came into the world. I don't. My story of my daughters' delivery is filled with fear, crisis, and unimaginable grief. In fact, it is not at all easy yet for me to even talk about my twins' delivery. It's too painful for me to discuss with most people. So I don't.

(4) *Celebration of the birth:* I have more sympathy cards than baby congratulation cards. I cherish the few celebration cards I did get. They may be hard to look at, but I'm glad I have them because they were given to me at a brief moment in time when both my girls were alive. They congratulated us on parenthood, which many people forgot to do.

(5) *Raising Twins:* I was so excited to be having twins. I had secretly dreamed of that my entire life. I knew well that it would be overwhelming at times, but I wanted very much to take on the challenge. The girls would always have each other. I looked forward to seeing the bond they would share as twins. Now, seeing anything twin-related is very hard on me. They are gut-wrenching reminders that Madison is not here, that I am not raising twins, and that Kaitlyn has been robbed of ever knowing her sister.

(6) *Seeing Madison grow up:* Madison is frozen in my mind as a one-pound baby. I was robbed of her ever growing up, and knowing all she would have become. I can list so many things I was robbed of, but it really can be summed up with just one word: "Madison."

Audra Losing Gabriel leaves me with a sense of being robbed of so many precious things: a full-term pregnancy, a normal delivery, and the joy of bringing my baby home. I feel particularly robbed of the milestones I anticipated enjoying with my son: him sleeping through the night, watching his first steps, teaching him his first words, photographing his first haircut, enjoying his birthdays, and all the lovely moments between and beyond. I was robbed of a lifetime of parenting him, and everything that journey would have brought: laughter, tears, worry, happy times, trying times, celebrations. Going on after being robbed of Gabriel is terribly hard. I must rebuild a life from what was left, and sometimes it seems very little is left on which to build. My family has been robbed of that which centered us.

Heather I have been robbed of happy pregnancy memories. Those excited, "nothing will go wrong, I'm doing everything I should, so bad stuff won't happen to me" feelings that other pregnant women have are completely lost on me. Because my labor came too soon and my son was born too early, my experience with his pregnancy and birth does not conjure feelings in me of awe at new life and new beginnings. Rather, my experience represents life lost, expectations shattered, hopes dashed. I was robbed of the happy, fulfilling birth experience of my child.

Death, tragedy, and grief are the replacements. But more important than a happy pregnancy, I was robbed of the life of my child. I will never know him, the color of his eyes or hair, the touch of his baby-soft skin, the joy of teaching him to walk or read or ride a bike, the joy of sharing a Christmas with him, and I will never see the child, teenager, and man he could have been. My saving grace is knowing that although I have been robbed of so much of what I wanted, my child has gained an everlasting peace in heaven. He will never experience this pain I feel now, and I am glad he has been spared that. I know that I will eventually join him in everlasting peace. There, I will have back what was taken from me here. And then I will finally get to know my son.

FEELING ROBBED

REFLECTIONS

FOR THE GRIEVING PARENT:
Do you feel a sense of being robbed? If yes, in what ways?

FOR THE FAMILY AND FRIENDS OF A GRIEVING PARENT:
In what ways do you see your loved one expressing a sense of feeling robbed? How can you better appreciate the reality of these feelings and convey that the feelings of being robbed are understandable and normal?

Vicky   What have I learned? Death does not come conveniently, nor does it adhere to our society's sense of fairness. Death is coldly indiscriminant, and leaves broken hearts angry and frustrated in its wake because there is no one to properly blame for the injustice of what has been lost. By nature, we wish to hold on tight to those we love, and we want to assign blame when something of ours is taken away. No wonder grief is so often expressed in anger, or in constantly repeating the words, "this isn't fair," or in trying to place blame. I suppose one healthy step in journeying through grief must eventually be to comprehend the hard learned truth that death is not so much a cruel thief as it is an undeniable part of life. We may try to deny for a long while that death will happen to us and to those we love. We may believe, for a portion of our existence, that we're all assured of being here tomorrow. But eventually the realities of death come to us all. I wonder if finding a sense of peace about death starts to come when one ponders less the injustice of what has been taken away…and ponders more the gifts graciously given.

THEME 3

Feeling Disconnected

Heather I've heard it said, "Your children are your window to the world." When Connor died, my window was slammed shut. A connection I so looked forward to—the wonders of friendships and experiences that raising a child would open up to my life—was denied. I feel completely disconnected right now from friends and acquaintances who have children. They are part of a wonderful club to which I want to belong but don't. They have gone on to breastfeeding, diapering, and sleepless nights, while I have gone on to walking empty-armed into sadness. When I watch my friends interact with their children, unfortunately all I can feel at this point is sadness. I know this will change eventually, especially when I have other children, but what I know right now is that it is an almost unbearable thing for me to watch a mother or a father nurturing their child, when I have lost mine. I watch them, and I know. I feel. I mourn what I am missing because my child is not here. The disconnect is felt on both ends of the relationship. Now people feel uncomfortable around me. For the first time in my life, I'm an oddity. They perceive me differently; they give me "the look." Most people don't know how to address this change. It is simply easier, simply more comfortable for them to ignore my situation, ignore my pain, and sometimes even ignore me.

Allison Everything changed the day Brennen died, especially me. I walked into the hospital that night one person, and I walked out of the hospital someone else. That night severed me from what I was before, knew before, and felt before.

(1) *I became disconnected from friends:* We are truly blessed to have many wonderful friends who showered us with cards, flowers, calls, and prayers. Yet since Brennen's death, I have never felt so utterly alone in all my life. I liken what I feel to living in a cage. People come to see me, pet me, feed me, talk to me…but nobody can free me. The worst part is looking out from my cage and seeing all the people who care for me, knowing they live freely from this grief of mine. It is not theirs to bear; it is mine. They don't understand the view from my cage and how deeply their casual conversations about potty training, daycare, or first words of other children cut into my heart. My son should be experiencing all this, but isn't. They don't understand how my heart cries when they will not mention or talk about my son unless I make them. Will they ever understand that I need to hear Brennen's name lovingly spoken? Why won't they even utter his name?

(2) *I became disconnected from my family:* I know that I am not the only one who lost someone that night. Brennen is a grandson, nephew, and cousin. Yet my family's pain is different from my own. In addition to the grief I feel as Brennen's mother, I also feel deep guilt for my family's pain. I cannot help but feel responsible in some way for their loss and their grief. As understanding as they are, they will never truly understand me, and how it hurts me so badly to hear them say, "Let's get the whole family together." Don't they know our whole family includes Brennen? Brennen is a part of our family, its history and heritage and bonds. It hurts me when this is forgotten or minimized. My family loves me, this I know and cherish, but they will never live with me in my cage.

(3) *I became disconnected from my husband:* Brian is truly, truly wonderful. I love him dearly. I couldn't have made it through all this without him. Yet he is a man, a father; I am a woman, a mother. How we feel and react is not the same. He doesn't un-

derstand the physical (C-section) scar on my belly runs deeper than my skin. Seeing it daily pierces my heart. He doesn't understand the guilt I feel for failing to carry Brennen safely into this world, which I tried so desperately to do for him and for our son. But Brian is the only one who fathoms how terribly much I miss Brennen. We share the depth of this in common. Although there are some things Brian doesn't understand because he is a man and I am a woman, he is the only one I feel connected to in my grief and who can enter my cage with me.

(4) *I became disconnected from myself:* Who am I now? Maybe it was necessary to disconnect myself from who I was before Brennen in order to deal with the pain after Brennen. I find myself thinking, saying, feeling, doing things I have never known before. New personality traits—jealousy, anger, shyness—are intense and very real in me now, where they never were part of me before. I didn't want to become this. I had no control over these things entering my life and heart and mind. But I have come to realize it's a part of who I am now, and I am learning to deal with it. I walked out of the hospital the night Brennen died, into my cage, and I changed.

Linda My grief has disconnected me from some people, but connected me to others, all of which has surprised me. After Madison's death, I quickly reached a point in which I was too weak mentally and emotionally to reach out to anyone. I was spent. I was numb. I needed my family and friends to reach out to me. But what I found is that many did not know what to do or say, so they didn't do or say anything. I did not have the energy to try to salvage whatever was there. A few true friends did reach out and were not afraid to be there for me, and for that I am extremely grateful.

I also feel strangely disconnected from most other mothers. With one surviving twin, I am in an odd place and find it hard to know where I can connect with other mothers. Most mothers cannot imagine my feelings about raising one daughter without her twin sister. Most freely talk with me about my surviving daughter, which I love, but when I mention Madison, they look at me with faces that say, "You mean you still think about the baby you lost?" I don't know what to do in those situations.

But mostly I feel cut off from Madison, and this is the worst disconnect of all. As time passes, the further and further I feel from her. I do not want to feel disconnected from Madison. I go to the gravesite often, so I can feel close to her, but I know her spirit and soul are not there. I hope Madison can feel my love in heaven, and I hope that I can feel connected to her again some day…forever.

Audra I feel as though I'm walking around lost in a fog. I can sense the world going on around me, but I can't make a connection with it. I feel different from everyone around me. I don't want them to see what's truly going on within me, because I'm tired of people trying to critique it. When I do attempt to reach out, I find I am often disappointed by the lack of understanding from people I thought would have a better grasp of my reality and more compassion. A lot of people keep their distance from me now, not knowing what to say to me or how to act around me. Sometimes that's good, sometimes that's bad. Luckily, I have a few close family and friends who have stayed connected to me. They are always open to listening to me and can comfort me without saying a word. I am truly grateful for these people in my life. I'm not sure where I'd be without them. However, I worry sometimes about putting too much on these few individuals and burdening them with my grief. I know it is heavy. So I try to distance myself from them at times for their well-being, because I don't want the weight of my grief to overburden them. But I can see them through the fog, never far off when I need them.

Tania A baby is not supposed to die, and when you are the parent left behind, there is such a wide open space between you and the rest of the world. We're "disconnected" from following what the world knows as the natural course of life. They've never even come up with a name for those of us whose babies die before us. We are not widows or orphans, so what are we? If our society can't even figure out a name to call us, how do we fit in with them anymore? There seems to be a big empty space between us and them. The empty space gets so big sometimes that I can't see anything else.

FEELING DISCONNECTED

REFLECTIONS

FOR THE GRIEVING PARENT:
Do you have feelings of being disconnected? If yes, from whom or what? What things can you do to help yourself: (1) stay connected to your baby, (2) feel okay about yourself during the time of disconnect with others, and (3) reconnect with others when you are ready?

FOR THE FAMILY AND FRIENDS OF A GRIEVING PARENT:
In what ways do you see your loved one struggling with feelings of being disconnected? How can you find ways to help them stay connected to their child? Are you allowing them the space and time they need when they are not ready to be around others (especially those with babies and young children)?

Vicky Our need to feel linked and bonded to one another is a universal desire in our human nature. Connection to fellow human beings is what gives us purpose, security, hope, and love in our lives. As the poem goes, no man is an island, set apart and isolated from other men. But, when death and grief hit, a terrible disconnect happens. This disconnect isn't just a bad feeling—it's an assault on a core human desire. For those experiencing the disconnect grief causes, is it any wonder they feel so very isolated, lost, alone, misunderstood, angry, and hopeless?

All of a sudden, through no fault of their own, they feel coldly set apart from the baby they loved, from the people they loved, and from the life they loved. So much of what they held precious is separated from them. What used to be comfortable to them is no longer comfortable. Death and grief have exiled them to a lonely island, and it takes monumental energy and courage to find their way off that island. But when that energy and courage is summoned up, and the griever finds a way back slowly into connectedness with fellow human beings again…that's when the healing begins.

Feeling Marked

Tania When I was in high school, I read *The Scarlet Letter* by Nathaniel Hawthorne where the letter "A" was the symbol splashed across the heroine's chest. I never expected in my life that I would walk around with my own symbol, my own mark. My mark is not sewn into my clothes; it is sewn into my heart. And others put it there.

When I went into early labor, people called me to see how I was doing and to see what happened. They asked things that shocked me, because they wanted to know what I had done to cause this early labor. Their questions accused me of causing my daughter's early birth, and they made me cry inside. Their questions told me they thought it was something I did, and that Lanika's arriving early was my fault. I feel like I have a big letter "K" forced on me. ("K" is for "Killer.") I did not kill my daughter. I did everything I could to save her. At first, I could not face these people and their questions. I could not bring myself to go out anymore, or face them pointing at me with their eyes. Then when I finally did go out, everyone spoke differently, looked at me differently. A "K" had been placed on me. I didn't belong anymore. I felt so lost. I am still lost, and I am trying to find my way.

Audra I feel like I am walking around with a big neon sign floating above my head that flashes: "The woman whose baby died," or "Fragile, do not touch." While I want people to know about Gabe and to remember him, I do not want to live with that burden over my head or to be defined like that. I want people to think of me as more than just that. I don't want people around me to constantly walk on eggshells and feel they have to watch what they say and do. I want them to know and treat me as the whole me, not just the part of me that is a mother to an angel.

Linda In the past, I placed marks on other people when I would think to myself, "Oh, she's the one with the disabled child," or "He's the one who has cancer." Now all of a sudden, I'm "the one," and I've learned it's a terrible feeling. I am uncomfortable in social settings because I feel like others look at me and think, "She's the one whose baby died." I have been marked by my family, my friends, my coworkers, and even by my doctor's office. People don't realize they're doing it, just as I did not realize I was doing it in the past. I know my grief makes me extremely sensitive, but it is a fact that people simply don't look at me the same anymore. They try hard not to let it show, but they are marking me. I see it in their eyes. Their mouths might never say, "Oh, you're the one whose baby died," but their eyes say loudly what their mouths do not.

Allison I feel like I wear my grief on my sleeve, and it makes me, my friends, and family very uncomfortable. I hate that I am now the person who walks into a room and suddenly people don't know what to talk about. I understand that my friends and relatives are struggling with how to act and handle this just as much as I am. But I feel like I am under the microscope—people watch me constantly to see if I'm upset or if I'm "recovering adequately." I am marked, and it's hard to know what to do when I am so painfully aware of people watching me to see how I feel. When

I am with friends and family, it's as if I wear a big fat "G" on my sleeve—they know I'm "Grieving," and so they "Gawk." This awkwardness of grief is almost as bad as the pain of grief. Most of the time, I find it much easier to be with strangers. They aren't expecting me to act a certain way or think I'm acting strange. I'm not marked in front of them, and they don't gawk at me. There is relief in that.

Heather When I first went back to work and began interacting with friends again after Connor's death, I felt my sadness was clearly visible and worn like clothing. It was always with me, and I was sure that everyone could see it, just like they could see the color of my shirt. I never thought I'd become "one of those sad stories," but I did. I was marked. People saw it, and would give me "the look." I think anyone who has experienced the loss of a baby knows what I'm talking about when I say "the look." It's the slightly cocked head, the sad, puppy-dog eyes, the slightly flattened lips, and maybe an accompanying sentence that only gets half-completed before it trails off to nowhere. It's a look that says they know, but they're afraid to really know. It's the look of pity. I hated "the look." I didn't want to be pitied, but every time I got "the look," I knew that's what it was. At the same time, I couldn't blame them for pitying me. I pitied myself. I was marked. And I did not like it.

Luckily, this all lessened over time, and my frustrations with it have changed to a hopefulness that something good may actually come from this marking. Maybe my being marked as the one who experienced the tragedy of losing my baby will eventually teach others something valuable. I can become a recognizable and approachable teacher or confidant about one of life's hardest lessons. Maybe my marking as a mother who delivered a premature baby who died will raise awareness in people that premature birth is a real societal tragedy for us all. Maybe my marking will wake Americans up into increasing efforts and funding more research to prevent premature birth. I want to turn this marking into something that will honor my son Connor. I do not want to be marked with "P" for "Pitied," or "D" for "Death." I want to be marked proudly with the letter "C" for "Connor," and all I do to honor him.

FEELING MARKED

REFLECTIONS

FOR THE GRIEVING PARENT:
Do you feel marked? If yes, in what ways and by whom? How much of what you feel is: (1) others marking you; or (2) you marking yourself? What do you think is a healthy way to deal with this feeling?

FOR THE FAMILY AND FRIENDS OF A GRIEVING PARENT:
Do you see your loved one bearing the discomfort of feeling marked in a crowd? How can you help prevent their sense of being marked or decrease their unease?

Vicky Grief following the loss of a baby dramatically increases a parent's level of sensitivity, especially when their grief is new, raw, and angry. Body language, facial expressions, certain words, questions, tones of voices, inflections placed on words, and awkward silences all take on new meanings to new grievers. This heightened sensitivity often causes pain—to grievers, and to their loved ones trying to help them. Grievers will often interpret things very differently than do the people around them. All of a sudden, they are affected deeply by seemingly subtle things—nothing in their lives seems subtle anymore. It's as if blinders have been taken off their eyes and hearts, and all wounds are totally exposed. They see more, feel more, and react more in the aftermath of losing a child. And while they can see pity, blame, avoidance, and watchful concern very astutely, I believe the saving grace is that they can also see care and love clearly as well. Grieving parents crave understanding, love, and touch (not pity, avoidance, advice, or blame). Tender loving gestures—a rub on the back, an extended hug, a pride-filled smile when an accomplishment has been achieved, an honest note that tells them someone cared about their baby and cares about them, a squeeze of the hand, a pat on the knee, a phone call on an anniversary date to acknowledge their loss—all speak volumes to grieving parents who feel marked and on display. They do not want to be an object of pity or blame. They just want their grief to be acknowledged, and then quite simply, they want to be loved. If this is what they experience, then heightened sensitivities subside over time, and the feelings of being marked and on display can slowly fade away.

Feeling Betrayed

Tania Feeling betrayed is something we humans often feel when things don't go our way and don't live up to our expectations. Losing my Lanika made me feel betrayed by God, family, my own body, and this world. I really can't control these feelings…. I tell you honestly that I feel them. I'm not proud of them, but they are there. I pray God will forgive me for feeling them.

I was not the only pregnant woman in the world at the time I carried Lanika…there were so many others pregnant at the same time I was. But when Lanika was born, I was separated from the healthy, fine pregnant women of the world who lined up in happiness. I was lined up in the row of sadness. I stood in a sad, tasteless, bland, colorless row. I was betrayed by the colorful world.

I always wanted a third child, but this pregnancy was unplanned. It was a gift from God, and I accepted it immediately with warm, happy feelings. I was so happy. As the days went by, I knew my friends and family would throw a surprise baby shower. I knew my two daughters would be very happy at the shower, celebrating their new sister's arrival. But life betrayed us on that. It was never ours. Then, when Lanika arrived, I felt she would be okay. I stored breast milk in the freezer for her, preparing to care for her when I brought her home. I started to dream about my life with three daughters. What a lovely dream it was. But my dream was wiped out when Lanika died. I looked in the freezer at all those bottles of breast milk and felt completely betrayed by God. I was doing everything to love this gift, and I did not understand how God could take her away from me. I am not upset at God anymore. I am just broken. My life is being glued back together, but I suppose the scars will always be there.

Allison Yes, I feel betrayed. I followed the rules, avoided the risks, and followed the doctor's advice to the last detail. And then my body betrayed me—the amniotic sac that protected my son broke too soon, denying Brennen the fluid his lungs required to develop. On the one hand, this experience has given me a heightened awareness of just how complex and intricate the creation of life truly is, and I am in awe of how many babies and families do make it through conception to birth with little or no complications. On the other hand, I find myself angry and frustrated: Why were we unlucky? I feel betrayed by God. I don't know how a rational person could avoid feeling betrayed. I constantly see on the news and hear stories at work of so many abused, abandoned, unwanted children, and I know that I would have done anything for just one more day with my son. Where is the sense in this? We are good, loving people. Why were my son and my family betrayed?

Heather I feel betrayed by my body. Now that I have gone through a second pregnancy and delivered a healthy, full-term baby, I wonder even more: Why did my body fail me during my pregnancy with Connor? Why did God betray me and take my child from me? I was very healthy: I did not have high blood pressure, an incompetent cervix, an infection, a uterine rupture, or diabetes. My water never broke. There is no known reason why I went into premature labor. I will probably never know why, but I wish so much there were an answer. If there were some answer to this mystery, maybe then I wouldn't feel so betrayed by God for not protecting my son, me, my husband, and my family from this terrible pain and grief. While I question God, I still very much believe in God's existence and goodness.

I also feel betrayed by those I expected to understand. I had a predetermined list of relatives and friends I assumed would grieve like I did, and when some of those on my list did not react like I expected, I felt betrayed. I am not proud that I felt this way, and it is hard for me to say this out loud, but I did. I need to talk about Connor, remember moments with him, cry about him, and acknowledge the fact that his life had a major impact on me. I assumed everyone on my predetermined list would understand all this, and I expected them to feel and act similarly to me. It seemed, from my perspective, life just went on for them as it always had before, and it made me question in frustration: Didn't Connor's life and death mean something, anything, to them? How could they forget and go on so quickly without him? Over time, I have come to realize that I set unrealistic expectations for most of my friends and relatives. I know now my grief is not the same as their grief. I am Connor's mother, and no one will grieve like I do. The strong feelings of betrayal that I felt initially have lessened considerably, but it has taken me a long time, a lot of crying, and a lot of soul searching to get here.

Finally, I feel that I betrayed Connor. I failed to bring him safely into this world. The most important job I will ever have will be to parent my children, and I failed at step one with Connor. To cope with this thought, I remember a quote a good friend shared with me: "Act as if it is all up to you but pray as if it is all up to God." I know I did everything within my power to bring Connor safely into the world, but ultimately, I know it is all up to God.

Audra I feel betrayed by my body. Try as I might, I could not control things that happened in my own body during my pregnancy. Wasn't it my job to do that? If I couldn't control it, then who was supposed to? I did everything I possibly could to have a healthy full-term pregnancy, but it was as if my body just turned against me.

I also feel betrayed by God. Throughout all of this, I was told to "Pray, pray for your miracle," and I did. My faith never wavered from believing God was going to carry my son and our family through this. One night, I sat alone in my silent car and pleaded with God to *please* make Gabe better and to take away his pain, because someone so small and so helpless did not deserve this. The next day, Gabe died. It was not the answer to my prayer that I wanted. I questioned: Why did someone so small, so innocent, have to suffer so greatly and die? If this was God's plan, then why should I pray at all? These are hard questions. I'm still searching for the answers…and I still pray.

Linda I really did not expect this part of grief—feeling so betrayed. I made early assumptions that significant people in my life would rally around and be there for me in this time of terrible tragedy and sorrow. Those I expected most to do this for me simply did not. It has been very hard for me to understand or accept this, and I feel betrayed by them.

On the other hand, there are many people who have come to our aid in our grief journey in the place of those who have run the other way. Brendan and I have received help and support from the most unexpected people, and we have been touched deeply by them. I believe this has been God's way of taking care of us throughout the hurt of our loss and the hurt of our betrayals. What is the word for the opposite of "betrayal?" Because we have experienced that as well.

FEELING BETRAYED

REFLECTIONS

FOR THE GRIEVING PARENT:
Do you feel betrayed? If yes, by whom or what? Which are strongest for you right now and the most difficult to deal with? Which of your feelings of betrayal might be based in unrealistic expectations or assumptions?

FOR THE FAMILY AND FRIENDS OF A GRIEVING PARENT:
Do you sense your loved one feels betrayed? If yes, by whom or what? Have you asked them what their expectations are of you and others in their grief journey?

Vicky There is a long litany of hurts in a parent's grief process. The first and most crushing hurt is the actual loss of their baby. But, as if that weren't pain enough for a person to endure, other hurts quickly follow for mothers and fathers after their child's death. The world and the heavens seem totally out of kilter to them. Nothing is as it should be. Because they sense so much has betrayed them, they are left feeling very confused. It is little wonder grieving parents despair and lose hope for the future. Their loved ones, God, and even their own bodies have let them down. As a result, they go through a period of deep questioning: Who and what can they ever count on again? When pondered, this is a very weighty question with many implications. I believe seeking and finding answers to this question can help tremendously in the search for peace. Who and what can really be counted on in life? Boiled down, everyone (not just a person who is grieving) seeks an answer to this fundamental question. To varying degrees, we are all "seekers" in life, trying to understand the meaning of our existence and in deciding who and what to trust as companions for our life journey. Experiencing a death tends to make a person a more motivated seeker because it brings many fundamental questions about life to the forefront. I believe there is a grace in this search, and a peace in the answers. One of the most stirring quotes in the Bible is: "Search, and you will find"—five very simple words packed with promise. Seeking the wisdom of God is what we're all called to do. Take note that we are told our wisdom is not of the same level as God's wisdom, and nowhere are quick answers to our questions promised. Therefore, faith and persistence will be essential in this lifelong search for understanding of God and God's ways. Bereaved people often become deep "seekers." We can greatly help grievers if we seek with them, finding along with them the answers about where to place our trust.

THEME 6

Crying

Tania My mom always used to tell me I cry a lot. She told me a tear was always waiting in the corner of my eye for action. It is true I cry a lot—I am very emotional. But right now in my life, my crying never stops. My husband thinks it's too much, but I cannot help it. I cry because it hurts….

> Lanika, dear, I'm crying 'cause I miss you
> crying 'cause I can feel you
> crying 'cause I need you
> crying 'cause I care.

Audra Tears are the little, salty badges of my emotions. They have surfaced for many different reasons over the whole course of Gabe's presence in my life. I cried when I found out I was pregnant—both from happiness and apprehension. I wanted a baby, but I wondered if I was ready and if I would be a good parent. I cried during my difficult pregnancy, every time a new issue arose threatening the life of my baby. I cried out of the fear and love I already felt for the life growing inside of me. I cried joyfully the day Gabriel was born, and when I saw my strong son fighting. I cried for the pain I saw him have to endure. I cried during our stay in the NICU: tears of frustration because all I could do was be a spectator to my son's fight, tears for every improvement he made and for every difficulty he encountered. I cried the day Gabriel died: tears of pain from losing the most precious thing ever in my life, tears of love in not knowing how to live without him. I still cry today: over the loneliness of my empty arms, over all the "what ifs," and over all the missed hugs and "I love yous." Sometimes I don't even know why I am crying, I just do. All these tears have one thing in common though—they are all tears of love for my son. And they have helped me get through this. They are the little salty badges of my love for my son.

Allison I was never a big crier, and crying in public was a rarity for me. Of course, that was before Brennen, and before I was filled with so much emotion that I had no other way to express it than through tears. I see much similarity between myself now and an infant child, where crying is the only means of communication. I have reverted back to the instinctual reflex of crying. It's the only way I can communicate some of my feelings. I remember waking myself up in the middle of the night shortly after Brennen died because I was sobbing uncontrollably and being held by my husband. In time, it did get better—I found more words and actions to express my emotions, and I needed tears a bit less. I understand the need to cry; it's an instinct and it serves a great purpose of release. What I don't understand though is how unpredictable and uncontrollable crying can be. I don't really understand why a simple comment can open my flood gates, while other times, when I'm really focusing on Brennen, tears don't come at all. I am confused by my crying, and sometimes I am embarrassed by it. All I know is that I really do need to cry, and so I do.

Linda It should be a "no-brainer" that crying needs to go with grieving, but our society sends out so many negative messages about crying. We are trained from early childhood that crying is not a good thing. We are told not to be crybabies. As we get to be teenagers, crying is seen as a sign of hormonal and emotional instability. As adults, crying is seen as a sign of weakness and vulnerability. Crying in the workplace is completely frowned upon. And crying for no apparent reason is seen as unstable. People have all kinds of ideas on how appropriate crying is when you're grieving:

- Crying "too much," long after the loss has occurred, is seen as "not moving on" with your life.
- Crying "too little," soon after a loss, is viewed as cold and callous.
- Crying "at inappropriate times" is viewed as being out of control.
- Not crying "at appropriate times" is seen as heartless.

People avoid any topic with me that they think could possibly bring me to tears. I want to tell everyone: Crying is *not* the worst thing in the world! When your baby has died, there is no such thing as crying too little, or crying too much, or crying at inappropriate times. Crying makes me feel better most of the time. Crying makes me feel close to Madison. Crying is a way for me to release some of the grief I'm drowning in, and shedding tears allows me to keep my head above water for a while. I do not want a person to apologize to me if they do say something that triggers my tears—my crying is not a crime. It helps me.

Heather Prior to Connor, I didn't have much reason to cry, and so I didn't very much. After Connor, I have hundreds of reasons to cry, and so I do very much. I believe I have cried more this last year than my entire life leading up to Connor. I cry for so many reasons: for failing to successfully bring Connor into this world healthy, for not getting a chance to really know him, for the pain I saw him suffer, for seeing my husband and family in grief, for the yearning I have for my son, and for the tragedy of it all. In the first months after Connor's death, I cried constantly, and I wondered if my tears would ever cease. It was exhausting, but crying made me feel better, and it was an excellent release. It brought relief when nothing else could.

I have learned that many are uncomfortable with crying, even some of those I thought I could trust with my tears. I wish I could be able to cry in front of everyone. That seems to me to be a more honest and healthy way to grieve.

As time has passed, I cry less frequently. However, I do not think this should be used as a gauge of how I'm dealing with my grief. Some of my friends and loved ones have tried to use the number of times I cry in a day, week, or month as an indicator of my "getting better" or "getting over" Connor's death. They wrongly assume that the fewer times I cry, the further along I am in the grief process and the closer I am to finally getting over it. While I appreciate their concern for me, I wish they'd realize grief just doesn't work this way. There is no magical way to measure the progress of a grief journey by counting crying episodes. Grief is too individualistic, too complex and dynamic, and too unpredictable to use a numeric "crying gauge." Sometimes I still cry several times a day or several times a week, and I feel better and healthier on those days and weeks than on those when I don't cry at all. Crying is a part of my life now. I embrace it because it helps.

CRYING

REFLECTIONS

FOR THE GRIEVING PARENT:
What makes you cry? Do you feel better after you've cried? Who are you comfortable crying in front of? Who are you uncomfortable crying in front of? How much has crying become a part of your life? Is there a particular place you feel safe in which to cry?

FOR THE FAMILY AND FRIENDS OF A GRIEVING PARENT:
How have you let your loved one know that they can feel comfortable crying in front of you? How have you encouraged or discouraged them to cry? What can you do to give your loved one a comfortable environment in which to cry when he or she needs to?

Vicky Photographers have a saying: "The eyes are the windows to the soul." By dabbling in portraiture over the past decade, I have come to find this adage to be very true. If you really want to capture the essence of a person in a photograph, focus on the eyes. God made "the windows to our souls" to include a built-in instrument for healing when our souls are hurting, and it is mostly water that flows from our eyes when we cry. What are the properties of water? Water cleanses, dilutes, washes away, brings life, clarifies, soothes, and refreshes. When you really think about it, isn't crying ingenious? What a blessing that we have this capability to shed tears when our lives become too much for us to handle. What would any of us (babies, children, adults) be like if we didn't have the ability to cry? When grieving the loss of a baby, surely opening the flood gates to the windows of our hurting souls for release, until we feel cleansed and soothed, must be monumentally important in the journey toward peace. Cry, my dear grieving friends, cry.

Triggers

Audra After the tragedy of losing a child, a parent sits exposed to the harsh elements of the world, and without much warning most of the time, something triggers intense feelings of sorrow and yearning. You try to protect and even desensitize yourself to these triggers, but often it's in vain. My triggers are confounding and inconsistent. Sometimes the things that bother me on a bad day slip past me on a good day. Some make easy sense, others don't. My triggers include:

- *Pregnant Women:* I fear for the expecting mothers that I see, and I do not want one more woman to go through what I did. At the same time, I am also jealous of pregnant women because not only are they pregnant (and I am not), but because they are naïve of the problems that could happen to them and to their child (and I am not).
- *Babies:* Anything at all to do with babies is always a reminder to me of what I had and what I was so close to having.
- *Music:* A song I used to listen to in the car on the way to visit Gabe in the hospital, or a song that we played at his funeral, can be a powerful trigger for me. Any song about love lost, missing someone, or losing someone can make my sad, yearning feelings rise to the surface.
- *Loneliness:* Whether actually being alone or just feeling alone, loneliness is a trigger for me. It is then when I have more time for thoughts, fears, pain, and tears to come pouring back. If Gabe were here, I know I would not be alone.

Heather My biggest trigger was my second pregnancy—up until twenty-four weeks gestation (the gestational age at which Connor was born). Everything during that time reminded me what it was like for so many key moments in Connor's existence: when I first learned that I was pregnant with him, when I had the first doctor's appointment, when I heard his heartbeat for the first time, when I saw him by ultrasound for the first time, when I learned his sex, and when I felt him move and kick. While the happy events in my second pregnancy were wonderful for my new daughter, and they were precious moments to me, they also triggered an extremely strong yearning in me for Connor.

Another big trigger for me is other children. This trigger has changed over time. At first, seeing children of any age hit me hard because they reminded me of what I was missing. It was hard to drive by a park in our neighborhood and see children playing. But as time progressed, the age limit dropped, and it was just young baby boys that triggered sad, yearning feelings in me. Hearing any baby cry was almost unbearable at first for me. And still today, every once in a while if I see a young baby boy who I think Connor would have looked like, I am taken back to a strong sense of sadness.

Other triggers for me include: watching a birth scene on TV, or some smells, sounds, or words that evoke memories of Connor. I miss him so much, and so many things remind me that I do.

Linda There are so many things I encounter that trigger memories of Madison and my grief for her loss. There are times that I wish I could avoid triggers all together and other times when I long for the triggers. Many of the triggers are unexpected and unavoidable—they usually hit me like a ton of bricks. There are too many to count, but I have listed a few of my most frequent triggers:

- *Music:* Brendan and I listened to music as a way to comfort ourselves in the months following Madison's death. Songs can still bring me to tears in a moment's time.
- *Pregnant women:* I just want to walk up to perfect strangers who are pregnant and tell them how very lucky they are.
- *Anything twin-related:* Twin clothing, twin strollers, TV shows about twins—that is what my life was supposed to be like. I was supposed to be raising twin girls.
- *Madison's name:* It's a very popular name right now, and whenever I see the name "Madison" embroidered or written on something, it brings up sad feelings in me.
- *Seeing Kaitlyn grow up:* With every milestone that Kaitlyn reaches, we celebrate her accomplishments. However we can't help but mourn that Madison never had the chance to achieve these milestones. We want to celebrate them both, and we can't.
- *Holidays:* Every day is hard, but holidays—when families are meant to be together—are the hardest. While everyone else celebrates, I spend the whole day missing Madison.
- *Hearing other moms complain about motherhood:* I don't want to hear anyone complain about being a mother or how hard it is. They don't know how lucky they are.

Allison Triggers of grief are like being on a strict diet and going shopping on an empty stomach. You're surrounded by the things you want, your body aches for them, but you just can't have them. Some of my triggers make sense (babies, birthday parties, hospitals), and I can prepare myself for them well in advance. Then there are others that pop up very unexpectedly and blindside me, and I find them the most difficult. These have been a few of my more unexpected triggers:

- *Getting dressed in the morning* and still having to wear my old maternity clothes after my baby was gone.
- *Follow up OB doctor visits* and sitting in the waiting room knowing I should be getting prenatal care, not post-partum care.
- *Dealing with insurance* for months and months after Brennen died. The only place I saw his name in print was on medical bills.
- *PMS*—having my body and my hormones go back to normal and having a monthly reminder that I am no longer pregnant when I am supposed to be.
- *Unexpected questions from unaware people*—store clerks, my middle school students, and neighbors sometimes ask questions like "How's the baby?" or "Is this your first child?" (when they see me with my second child) or "How many children do you have?" These people are totally unaware of what happened to Brennen and what my situation is. I don't want to ever deny that Brennen existed, and I feel strongly about always answering truthfully, but then do these people really want to know my truth? I am still trying to determine a game plan for these types of situations, but there's not an easy answer.

Tania Allah made us all with a big heart, but we don't seem to know how big our heart really is until it is broken, until everything around us triggers the feelings of love we have for the people who filled us with so much happiness. Triggers for me are both bitter and sweet. Some make me laugh, others make me cry. Birthdays, holidays, and anniversaries are my biggest triggers.

We are supposed to celebrate life and families at these times, and we have much to celebrate. When my other girls have their birthdays, I am so happy with them. But their times of rejoicing in life trigger me to think about Lanika, who won't ever get to celebrate with us. I close my eyes and think what she would be doing right now if she were with us, what her two sisters would be doing with her if she were here. I laugh and cry as I think. I never realized how big my heart is or how perceptive my eyes are before Lanika died. Now my eyes see things they never saw before, and my heart is triggered by the love I have within it.

TRIGGERS

REFLECTIONS

FOR THE GRIEVING PARENT:
What triggers your grief? How do you handle the expected triggers that you know are coming? How do you handle the triggers that come unexpectedly, don't make much sense, and blindside you?

FOR THE FAMILY AND FRIENDS OF A GRIEVING PARENT:
Have you asked your loved one what triggers their grief and what they do or do not feel comfortable being around right now? Which of their triggers seem understandable to you? Which are not understandable to you? Have you adjusted your expectations of your loved one to give her or him time to learn to handle their triggers, whether or not you can relate to them?

Vicky   The death of a baby is a singular event in the life of a parent, but their grief is perpetual. All five of these women have told me they replay the moments of their baby's lives and deaths repeatedly in their minds, and that they cry for their babies in their sleep. They can't control these things—they just happen. Audra, Heather, Linda, Tania, and Allison all tell me that they know on their own deathbeds they will be thinking and talking about their babies who died. These mothers describe to me survival tactics they've learned of "putting on their armor" or their "game face" every time they go out in public. It takes great courage to re-enter the world after the devastating loss of a baby, and these mothers take very deliberate actions to walk the steps of grief in a world that mostly misunderstands their journey. What is going on inside these grieving mother's minds and hearts is often not really reflected by their outward appearance. But periodically, a trigger pierces their armor and takes them right back to the life and death moments they had with their babies. When this happens, any of the emotions they experienced while their child was with them can be relived: sadness, joy, fear, guilt, pride, confusion, love, etc. Triggers are conjured by all the senses. Sights, smells, sounds, tastes, and touches can all instantly transport a parent back to the times they had with their babies. I believe triggers are proof that we humans love with our whole minds, bodies, and souls. It is no cliché that once a loved one leaves us in death, we carry on with them in our hearts forever. We continue to love them with our minds, bodies, and souls. It is the way of love.

THEME 8

Guilt

Tania Guilt is a very difficult thing to deal with after your baby dies. While guilt is normal and universal, it is hard to understand. I know that the guilt I feel over Lanika really makes no sense. It leaves more questions than answers. I know in my head I should not feel guilty, but then why do I? I don't believe in my head that Lanika's death was my fault, but why do I wonder what I could have done differently? Although I know I took care of myself the best I could, why do I question that I didn't do enough? I question everything: Maybe I shouldn't have cleaned the house that one day, or lifted that box, or had that argument with my husband, or let them take my baby away so quickly after she died. Right after Lanika died, I rejected the opportunity to have our picture taken with her. I regret not having photos of her or our family together. But in reality, would changing any of these behaviors really have made what happened any different? Of course not. Nothing I could have done would have changed the fact Lanika came early and that she died. I did everything I could for Lanika. Common sense tells me not to feel guilty. And yet that lingering guilt still makes me question…everything.

Linda Guilt comes in waves. It ebbs and flows like the surf against the shore. Sometimes huge tides of guilt suck me under, and it's difficult to breathe. Other times, they're just small waves and I can handle them. While I know that Madison's early birth and death were not my fault, I battle with guilt. I have so many questions. Shouldn't I have known something was wrong? Why didn't I know? On the day of the girls' births, why didn't I go to the hospital sooner? I have since found that there is a possible link between periodontal disease and pre-term labor. I was treated for my periodontal disease with two cleanings during my pregnancy. Did I cause their early birth because of my illness and the treatments for it? If I had just taken care of this before I got pregnant, maybe the outcome would have been totally different. Why didn't I know this?

During my darkest moments of guilt, a little voice tells me, "You killed your baby!" Even though I know this is not true, the voice is very convincing because it's my own voice speaking to me. That is why I immediately have to confront these overwhelming waves of guilt with the truth. I did everything I knew how to do. I did not kill Madison. There was so much I simply didn't know, and my doctors didn't know. There were no indications for us to do anything differently to prevent the eventual outcome. I did everything I knew to do for Madison, and I hope somewhere up there in heaven she knows that.

Heather I am conflicted between guilt and common sense. On one hand, I know logically that Connor's early birth and death were not my fault, but I sometimes feel totally responsible. At first, I couldn't help but replay the day I went into early labor over and over in my mind, wondering if there was something, *anything*, I could have done differently that day or in the weeks leading up to that day. It was my job to nurture and protect Connor inside me— his coming early was my ultimate failure. When he struggled in the NICU, I was hopelessly inadequate as a mother to protect him and to spare him the suffering I saw him endure. Why couldn't I have done more for my son? Wasn't that my job? If I had known to do anything differently, I would have.

I haven't talked too much with others about my guilt outside the Good Grief Group and my husband. It's an emotion that really hurts. Audra, Linda, Tania, Allison, and Vicky understand. Cole patiently reminds me that I didn't do anything wrong, and that this is not my fault. Rationally speaking, I know I would have done anything to prevent our trip to the NICU and Connor's death, and that is how I am able to deal with this guilt. I know I couldn't go on living a productive, happy life if I really owned this guilt. It isn't logical and it isn't healthy. And so, I try to let it go.

Allison Literally minutes after we were told of Brennen's death, doctors, nurses, family members, and friends were all telling me that his death was not my fault. They told me I had done absolutely everything I could have done for my son. I know their intensions were to comfort and reaffirm, but in actuality, it had the complete opposite effect on me. They knew exactly what my thoughts as Brennen's mother were. Everyone around me knew just as I did that it was my job to give Brennen a healthy entry into this world. It was my role to carry him. I was the only one who could deliver him into the world. I was the one who failed him.

So yes, I have carried a great deal of guilt in my heart as I have grieved Brennen's death. But my guilt does not consume me, because I know that all the choices I made surrounding his pregnancy, birth, and life were all to give him the best possible chance for survival. I know I did everything that I could and should have done. I know that in a trial of my peers, nothing would be found against me to charge me as guilty. Yet I am—I plead guilty! My body failed my son. His life was my responsibility, and I couldn't give Brennen everything he needed to survive. It hurts to know this.

After all these months since Brennen's death, I still feel guilt, but it has changed over time. I have moved forward with life, and now the guilt tends to be more focused on feeling guilty about moving forward without him. There is discomfort in me knowing my precious son, my Brennen, is left behind. I still feel responsible for him in some ways. Now it's up to me to keep his spirit and memory alive. When I do, and others around me join me in doing this, I feel better.

Audra Guilt is grief's twin—the two seem to come hand in hand. Whereas certain things trigger my tears, other things trigger my guilt. I know I didn't do anything wrong, and so I know there shouldn't be any guilt…but I felt so responsible for Gabriel. I know doctors and nurses also hold a lot of responsibility for NICU babies, and they do everything they possibly can to save them. But at the end of the day, those babies were just their patients. They can walk away from it. At the end of my day, Gabe was my son, and I can't just walk away from it. He was my ultimate responsibility, not theirs. And so guilt lingers in me, and will probably linger indefinitely.

Guilt is a bit of a moving target, taking on new forms as life goes on. At first, when I was pregnant with Gabriel, I felt "body guilt" because I couldn't control the things happening in my body that ultimately led to his premature arrival. Then as he suffered in the NICU, I felt strong "maternal guilt" because I couldn't keep bad things from happening to my son. After he died, I felt strong "family guilt." I saw how his death affected members of my family, and I felt guilty about their hurt and how family relationships were affected by it all. Then as time went on, I began to experience "going-on guilt." I felt guilty about going on in my life without him. Going on puts me further and further away from him, and that makes me feel guilty. Then as hope and joy came back into my life, I experienced "happiness guilt." Sometimes when I would laugh and enjoy myself, it somehow would translate in my head that I wasn't being faithful to or honoring Gabe. He was dead and gone: How could I ever laugh or be happy again? More recently, I have felt "remembrance guilt." It comes whenever I sense I'm not doing enough to remember and honor my son. I always have a sense that Gabriel is up in heaven looking down on me, watching me. Just as I wanted to do right by him when he was alive, I want to do right by him after his death. And as crazy as this must sound, I experience "no guilt" guilt. If I go a while without sensing guilt about Gabriel, then my mind starts to wonder if I'm forgetting about him. I literally can feel guilty for not feeling guilty.

As time has gone on, I wrestle less with guilt than I used to. I don't let myself dwell on guilty thoughts; I try always to remember the truth. And I think as Gabe looks down on me, he'd be okay with that.

GUILT

REFLECTIONS

FOR THE GRIEVING PARENT:
Do you struggle with guilt feelings over the loss of your baby? Where does truth lie—about what was within your ability to do for your baby and what was beyond your control? Can you determine who is making you feel guilty— you or someone or something else? What ways have you found to let go of your guilt?

FOR THE FAMILY AND FRIENDS OF A GRIEVING PARENT:
Has your loved one ever expressed to you their guilty feelings over the death of their baby? How can you allow them to articulate these thoughts without them feeling uncomfortable or judged?

Vicky Few other times in life do we experience such a strong sense of responsibility as when we become parents. How does this tremendous sense of responsibility concerning parenthood develop? Our culture, upbringing, and religious beliefs intertwine throughout much of our lives to define what we expect of ourselves as parents. No matter what background one has, most would agree that parenting is quite possibly the most important function most of us will ever serve in this world. Audra, Heather, Linda, Tania, and Allison, as do most other new mothers, welcomed the duties of motherhood with excitement and felt extremely responsible for their babies. These five women lovingly fulfilled their jobs as protectors and nurturers to their babies to the full extent of their ability. But in each of their babies' lives, something went terribly wrong. Despite their best efforts to nurture and protect, these women watched helplessly as their babies suffered and died. Their strong sense of responsibility collided with terrible life events over which they had no control. And now in the aftermath, there is guilt.

On some days, their guilt is subtle. Other days it rages, completely overwhelming them. These mothers know the indisputable fact that they were not responsible for their baby's death… and yet, they feel guilt. Why? Hearing repeatedly that their babies' deaths were not their fault (from trusted doctors, nurses, friends and family) does not alleviate their guilt. Why not? On the one hand, they believe their guilt is not logical because they know (intellectually) that they did absolutely nothing wrong. But, on the other hand, their guilt is totally understandable because (emotionally) parents often expect superhuman abilities of themselves in the quest to protect their child from every harm. Guilt is therefore an emotion not based in logic.

So what is a grieving parent to do with the nagging guilt? I believe this is an instance in life where logic and emotion are too busy battling one another for either to be helpful. Instead of logic or emotion, I believe grieving parents must rely on faith as a way to deal with guilt. When the nagging questions persist ("Why didn't I do this?" or "Why couldn't I have stopped that?), the beautiful words from John's Gospel may help:

"You will know the truth, and the truth will make you free."
John 8:32

Battle the questions with truth because the truth is clear: Biology, or even medical science, failed your baby, but you did not. Make a conscious effort to put the onus where it rightfully belongs, and let the truth set you free of your guilt. When the nagging, self-reproaching thoughts start up in your mind ("I killed my baby" or "This is all my fault" or "I should have done more"), John has more beautiful words to ponder:

> *[God] will reassure our hearts before him*
> *whenever our hearts condemn us;*
> *for God is greater than our hearts,*
> *and he knows everything.*
> 1 John 3:19-20

Battle the self-condemning thoughts with the knowledge that no one, not your partner, nor your baby, and especially not God, finds any parental deficiency in you. Make a conscious effort to accept that the death of your baby was the result of misfortune, not the result of any deficiency in you.

THEME 9

Grieving Mothers and Grieving Fathers

Allison Unquestionably, Brian and I have handled our grief over Brennen's death much differently. We each assumed different roles in the difficult pregnancy—Brian became the supporter, and I became the incubator. I think those roles and expectations established early on in the pregnancy carried over into the aftermath of Brennen's death.

We both feel guilt. I feel completely responsible for Brennen's unhealthy arrival, as though I let everyone down—my baby, my husband, and our families. This has made me very sensitive to certain passing comments and gestures. Brian, on the other hand, feels guilty for not taking full advantage of some of the days that Brennen was with us and for missed opportunities.

I have become jealous and resentful towards women who have or can have healthy babies. I avoid being around them still. Brian doesn't avoid the joy of other families like I do. He celebrates their joys with them, not wanting to miss out on the special moments of life and family.

I am easily overcome by emotion, but I mostly welcome the tears because I know they come from my deep love for my son. Brian keeps a strong exterior, and rarely allows his sad emotions to show. He had to go back to business as usual at work soon after our world and dreams fell apart. Emotions are not shown by men at work, so he didn't. He wants to show strength to me so that he can hold me up on sad and hard days.

I have grown stronger and more dedicated in my faith. I feel my connection with God helps me stay connected with my son. Brian has questioned his faith.

I feel a deep need to remember my son and have him remembered by others. I want to share his story with anyone who feels comfortable listening to it. Brian only shares Brennen's memories with a select few.

No one is wrong or right here. We're each finding our way to deal with our situation. Despite how differently Brian and I express our feelings and emotions, we both feel the loss. We help each other through our differences, and we help each other see the blessings our son gave us. We help each other grieve as we each need to in order to continue to love, live, and dream again.

Tania My husband is very quiet in general, and he never says anything about Lanika. I wish he would. But I know talking is not his way, and I have to accept how he is. It doesn't mean he doesn't love Lanika, it just means our ways are different. I need to talk it out, and he lets me. I love to tell the whole world how she was, that she was a princess. I really don't know what is in a grieving father's heart, because my husband hasn't told me yet. I can only guess right now about how it is full of pain. I hope some day my husband will tell me, so some day I will know his pain, he will know mine, and we will find peace together.

Audra Erik and I dealt with things very differently during Gabriel's life and death. Erik's needs and ways of communicating were polar opposites of mine. When Gabe died, I needed to do things that reminded me of him. Erik did not see value in me doing this. He thought I was wallowing in my grief. We never really learned to communicate our needs to each other. Our miscommunication led us down different roads after Gabe died. Unfortunately, we were divorced by the anniversary of Gabe's second birthday.

Heather Cole and I grieve in very different ways. At first, this actually made me angry, but I came to realize there is no one "right way" to grieve the death of a baby. Grief is very unique to an individual, and especially different between most women and men.

My grief is very visible. I am quick to cry, I need to talk about it, and I can sometimes let myself be seen as vulnerable. Cole keeps his grief more insulated. He is not comfortable crying in front of anyone, and he rarely cries in front of me. I think he does this for two reasons: (1) he really needs private moments to cry, and (2) he is trying to protect me from his grief and any further hurt. I rely on Cole to support me. I am comfortable crying around him and do so frequently. I feel guilty about this—he helps me through my down moments, but who is there for him? Anytime he does share with me, I cry for his hurt. I feel so terrible for him. It is hard for me to see the man I love so much in pain. Then he feels bad, thinking he has made things worse for me. We each hate to see the other crying and hurting. It's a vicious cycle, and I really don't know the right way out of it.

What I do know is that Cole loves Connor as much as I do. We both lost our firstborn, our son. We both had dreams shattered for that child. We both lost someone we wanted in our lives. Cole internalizes his grief, and I externalize mine. He is my best friend, and I couldn't have survived this loss without him holding me. Our marriage is stronger for having taken this journey together, side by side.

Linda Men and women in general handle grief differently. I know I have been fortunate in that Brendan is quite open to showing his emotions and talking to me about losing Madison. I tend to talk more about it than he does, but I know that doesn't mean she's not on his mind. It's the little things he does that help me know this.

Madison's gravesite is close to our home, and Brendan and I both pass the cemetery almost daily. We have a vase in her headstone that we always try to fill with fresh flowers. Every time either one of us goes out there, we take the old, dead flowers out and replace them with a fresh bouquet. It's the only thing we can buy Madison. It makes us both feel good to do it. Sometimes I will see dead flowers in the trash and I will know Brendan has been out to the cemetery to visit her grave and give her new flowers. While I'm sad that he has to even do this, it warms my heart to know he visits her grave without me, on his own, and buys her flowers. This means more than anything he could say because it shows me how much my daughter is loved by her father.

While we are slightly different in our outward emotions in expressing our grief, I know that our hearts feel the same loss, feel the same pain, and that we both cherish Madison equally.

GRIEVING MOTHERS AND GRIEVING FATHERS

REFLECTIONS

FOR THE GRIEVING PARENT:
How have you and your partner grieved differently for the loss of your child? How have you grieved similarly? How do you communicate and support one another in your differences?

FOR THE FAMILY AND FRIENDS OF A GRIEVING PARENT:
In what ways do you see the mother and father grieving differently? How can you support both the mother and the father in their own unique expressions and thoughts of grief?

Vicky Grief expresses itself differently between genders. Just as most husbands and wives maintain their cars differently, enjoy sports differently, spend time with best friends differently, approach housecleaning and yard work differently, and relate to children differently, they approach grief differently. The fact of the matter is they each need to find healthy ways to grieve. Sometimes there is overlap with one another and common ground in grief, sometimes there is not. As hard as the death of a child is on a family unit in general, it becomes even more complex when poor communication festers and unrealistic expectations are placed on one another in the grief journey. The death of a baby is terribly difficult on a relationship and marriage. If the mother and father are to successfully journey toward peace in their grief, they each need to feel understood and held up by the other. They need to effectively communicate with one another. If I had any advice to give to grieving mothers and fathers, I would say: Share tender gestures between one another, appreciate how the other must express themselves, set aside time to attend to your grief in healthy ways together, don't unload your grief anger on one another, rebuild your plans for the future together, and walk next to one another radiating strength to one another...hand in hand.

Insensitive Comments, Assumptions, and People

Linda I have learned a painful lesson as I have journeyed through my grief: People in modern American society are very ignorant about grief. I readily admit, I too was ignorant before all this happened to us. In our culture, we don't hear, experience, or learn much about the realities of death and grief, and therefore we are largely ignorant of it. Plainly and honestly put, we Americans are stupid about grief, and it leaves the grieving to endure unhelpful comments and assumptions that people around them make about it. I have been surprised to learn that not only do I have to endure the unbearable loss of my child, but I also have to find a way to endure our society's general ignorance of what grief truly is. In my case, many people discounted my grief over Madison because they felt I should have been happy enough to have Kaitlyn.

My advice to those trying to console the grieving:

- Never start a sentence with the words "At least…" There is nothing, and I mean nothing, "at least" about losing a child.
- Never say you know how they feel. You don't.
- Don't assume a lifetime of worry over a disabled or seriously sick child would have been worse than the death of a child.
- Don't give advice on how to grieve unless you're asked.
- Know that words do little to make a grieving parent feel better. Your actions toward them will do much more than words could ever do.

Tania When something happens in our lives that deeply affects us, we want everyone around us to think like us. But I have learned they don't. I have learned that words which come out of other people's mouths about my loss and my grief hurt. I don't want to listen anymore to them, because their words just make me cry.

Yes, people say insensitive things. Some come from "insiders" (family members and good friends) and some come from "outsiders" (coworkers and casual acquaintances). The thoughtless comments from insiders hurt the most. I guess I wrongly assumed they would know better.

Someone very close to me told me one day that this all happened because of me. I did not want to believe my ears. I felt like the ground was moving away from under my feet. If *this* person didn't understand, who would? I was the one who shared my body willingly and lovingly with Lanika all those months. I was the one who felt her move and come alive in me. I waited every second to feel her every movement. As long as I breathed, I wanted Lanika to have breath too. Now that she is gone and no longer breathes, I can hardly breathe myself. How could this person, this insider, think my Lanika is dead because of me?

I know people don't mean to hurt me by their words. I know they are really trying to help. Please don't say anything if you don't know how to love me through this grief. It's better if you just come be with me and don't talk.

Allison Before Brennen, I was a person who was uncomfortable around those in emotional turmoil. In all honesty, I would have had no clue as to what to say to a parent who experienced the death of their baby. I know that I cannot be overly upset with people who say ignorant things to me. They've never lived what

I've experienced. They're out of the realm of my knowledge and insight. I don't see these people so much as ignorant; I see them as lucky. They don't know the lessons I've learned. People are not deliberately and intentionally hurting me with their words. But the sad fact is: They do. Comments that have particularly cut to my heart:

- **"This is for the best."** I want to know: Whose best? Do they think it is best that Brennen never got a chance to grow up, and that Brian and I go through all this hurt? How is this best?
- **"Brennen's in a better place now."** Brennen's remains are cremated and in a wooden box now. How is that better than Brennen being in my loving arms?
- **"You're young.** You can have more children." The people who say this to me are missing the point altogether—I will never have Brennen, and that's what matters to me right now. I hope that someday I will have other children, but they will not bring Brennen back to me.

Audra I have found that people who've never experienced suffering in their lives often don't understand the suffering of others. In my dealings with people, before I interact with them, I have to: (1) evaluate where I'm at that day with my grief, and (2) whether or not the person is "worth my energy." It takes so much heart energy to open myself up to people and show my grief that I have learned to be cautious. I have been sorely disappointed at times when I surmised that a person would understand and act compassionately towards me, and then doesn't. I have to just let it go when this happens, otherwise I would be angry all the time. And I don't want to be angry all the time. Because of earlier life challenges I've had to deal with, I came to this grief already somewhat equipped with a few helpful coping skills on how to handle the insensitivity and harshness of the world. I experienced it then, and I'm experiencing it again now.

Because I was twenty-three when Gabe died, many friends and family tried to minimize my grief, saying that I could have more children. But that's totally beside the point. I want Gabriel.

One day a close friend, someone who knew my story well, said to me, "You'll understand when you have kids someday." I have had a child: He lived sixty-two days and taught me so much about life and living and parenting. My friend's comment coldly discounted all of this, and it hurt.

I prefer to spend time with people who are wise to suffering, who don't voice their opinions of my grief, and who just listen to me.

Heather I find it strange to hear people say, "I don't want to talk to you about Connor because I don't want to remind you of him, make you cry, or make you feel worse." Why do they think I don't want to be reminded of my beloved son? Why do they think crying is bad, or that I'm not crying anymore for him? I carry Connor in my heart at all times, he is always somewhere on my mind, and I will always remember him whether someone talks to me about him or not. My advice to those trying to help me: You don't need to try to find common ground with me—it's really not necessary, and when you try, often you make insensitive comments, and it hurts me.

I think that the coldest, least compassionate statement anyone could ever make is, "It was for the best." How could anyone think it's best my child died? But nearly as insensitive is anything that discounts the life of my child. Comments like, "You can always have another" or "How does it feel to finally be a parent?" (when a subsequent child is born) make me feel like my baby is forgotten, that his life never mattered or meant anything.

But I lived a lifetime with Connor.

Fortunately, I have found comfort in some beautifully compassionate, reassuring words. Some of the more comforting statements spoken to me include:

- "I can't imagine how you must feel."
- "I know your baby meant the world to you."
- "I will always remember your baby, and I am setting out with a new purpose in my life because of the impact his life had on me. I have also learned from your experience."
- "Cry all you want in front of me. It will not make me uncomfortable."
- "You were a wonderful parent to Connor."

INSENSITIVE COMMENTS,
ASSUMPTIONS, AND PEOPLE

REFLECTIONS

FOR THE GRIEVING PARENT:
Have you experienced insensitive comments, people, and assumptions? If yes, describe them and how they made you feel. How did you react? What might be a healthy way for you to handle these situations in the future?

FOR THE FAMILY AND FRIENDS OF A GRIEVING PARENT:
Name situations when you have seen your grieving loved one hurt by an insensitive comment, person, or assumption. How can you help them when you see this happen? How can you make sure you're not saying or doing something that will be hurtful to them at this time?

Vicky Our society's general lack of real understanding about the grief process puts an extra and very heavy burden on newly grieving parents. Unfortunately, they must also endure the sometimes hurtful words and assumptions of well-intentioned friends, family, and acquaintances. Even though the grieving person is battling great anger and rage within their heart over the terrible unfairness that their baby has died, they often find themselves in situations where they must take the higher moral ground with insensitive people. Time and again, grieving parents hear and experience very hurtful things, and then most often silently forgive those who do not understand the actual wounding effect of their words and actions. Many friends and family members seem to fumble awkwardly as they try to find golden words for grievers. But if words about the deceased child don't clearly tell the grieving parent that the child was welcomed lovingly into this world, lived too short a time, was dearly cherished, was highly significant, and is sincerely missed, then the words are better left unspoken. In fact, in the very early months of grief, I think the less said the better. A loving presence is stronger and more appreciated than any words.

If you truly want to comfort a grieving parent, be there for them. Cry with them, hug them, take a walk with them, listen to them, remember their child with them, hold their hand. Give them your time, not your opinions. In time they may want to know your opinion. Wait to give it until they ask for it. I believe there is a very good reason we are given two ears but only one mouth. Listen to the grieving—they need to be heard. Realize that when a baby dies, there are very, very few words of wisdom that can make a parent feel better about the loss of their beloved child. Don't fumble uncomfortably trying to offer them words of wisdom—simply admit you don't have any. Grievers will appreciate your honesty.

Communicating with Family and Friends

In watching the Good Grief Group struggle with insensitive comments, assumptions, and people, I surmised that a lot of what precipitated the uncomfortable experiences boiled down to two things: (1) society's general lack of understanding of parental grief, and (2) poor communication. On one side of the situation, there are grieving parents who are often confused, withdrawn, angry, and ineffective in communicating their needs. And on the other side, there are often loved ones who don't really understand the grief of the parent and are trying desperately to help, but often find themselves rebuffed. They walk away from their attempts to assist the grieving parent feeling criticized, unappreciated, and ineffective. After a baby dies, often what is left behind is a terribly awkward scenario for everyone involved. It is as if grieving parents and many of their significant family and friends have suddenly been uprooted and displaced to a strange, hostile country, and no one knows what to do anymore. No one knows the proper language to use with one another, or how to adjust together to the new reality—not the grievers nor those who love them. It totally disorients everyone involved. What can help this difficult situation? The answer, I think, lies in honest, non-judgmental, compassionate communication. So I asked the Good Grief Group at our gathering, after we finished our discussion about insensitive comments, assumptions, and people to:

- Identify their loved ones with whom they have the most trouble communicating.
- Identify reasons why the communication is so hard right now.
- Consider the experience, feelings, and perspectives of their loved ones in the aftermath of their baby's death.

Then I suggested to the mothers that they write a letter to their loved ones. I wanted them to find a way in a letter to clearly state what they as grieving parents feel, need, and don't need right now. The ladies loved the idea, and saw great potential in how this could be extremely helpful in their situations, but they quickly found themselves stuck in not knowing where to begin. In the end, they decided to work as a group and share ideas, and they came up with one letter they collectively wrote that expressed what they felt needed to be said. When their letter was done, they all agreed that something like this could have really helped them at the earlier stages in their grief journey and decreased many of the insensitive comments and assumptions they endured. They wish they had written this letter much sooner and mailed it to key people in their life.

What follows is Audra, Heather, Linda, Tania, and Allison's letter. We offer it to grieving parents as a suggestion, especially newly grieving parents. Maybe a letter would help you work through some of the difficulties in communicating with your family and friends since the death of your baby. Use this as an example to start with — read our letter, but then craft your own that fits your experience and needs. Our letter is written from a mother's perspective, but it can easily be adapted to express a couple's point of view. And to the loved ones trying to assist grieving parents, we hope reading this letter will help you in learning some of what helps, what hurts, and what can keep the communication lines open between you and your grieving loved one.

THE GOOD GRIEF GROUP'S LETTER
TO FAMILY AND FRIENDS

My Dear Family and Friends,

The past few weeks since my baby died have been the most difficult days of my life. I wanted to make sure you each knew how very much your love and support has meant to me, how much I appreciate all your kindness. I could never do this alone. Having you beside me, encouraging me through this terrible time, has helped me with the overwhelming grief I am experiencing. I can never express in words how much I appreciate and love you. Thank you from the depths of my heart for the vast outpouring of care given to me.

But there is more I need to say to help our relationship, which means so much to me, survive this difficult time when communication seems so difficult. Maybe if I share with you what I feel in my heart right now, we can not only get through this confusing time together, but our relationship can grow stronger.

Right now, I am emotionally drained, confused, angry, deeply sad, and totally exhausted. As a result, I really don't even know what exactly to ask from you, other than your unconditional love. I know that's a lot to ask. I'm not used to all these new things happening inside me now, so I can imagine they will bewilder you too. As I go through this grief journey, I know it will get better, and I will find my way, but I ask for you to be patient with me until that time comes. I recognize that my grief has made me self-absorbed right now, and I apologize if this has hurt you in any way. It's not something I can really help, and I truly don't mean to offend. But my current emotional capabilities are consumed in self-preservation, in caring for my husband and surviving children, and in trying to put the pieces of my heart and life back together. I won't always be like this, but for right now, your world has kept spinning, and mine has completely stopped. It will take me time before my world starts to spin again.

It seems that at a time when you and I most need to communicate, we are having trouble knowing just what to say to one another. We can't seem to find the right words. But please know: Fewer words in exchange for a listening ear are what I crave right now anyways. If you feel yourself struggling to know what to say to me, that's okay. I don't expect you to know. Just tell me you don't know, and then let's be comfortable together in silence. I need you more than I need words. Take a walk with me, cook a meal with me, let me talk about my baby with you, but don't be uncomfortable if a lot of words aren't shared right now. I'm fine with that. In time, I know words will come back.

Please realize I'm going to be different in some ways. I'm more sensitive to some things now than I ever was before, and I am not interested in doing all the same things I did before. My baby's death has changed how I look at the world, life, and love, and the change in me may create some unease between us. I don't want you to "walk on eggshells" around me; I want us to remain comfortable together. So maybe if I plainly tell you the things that are most difficult for me right now, you'll know how to be more at ease around me. Right now, I cannot find a way to be in situations that celebrate motherhood and children without becoming extremely saddened. Birthday parties, talk of pregnancies, holidays, baby showers, sitting in cars with car seats, and seeing parents strolling their babies only remind me painfully of what I am without now. So if I can't experience these things with you for a while, please know my actions are not a reflection of how I feel towards you, your child, or your family. I love you and am very happy for you all. But I need more time for my emotional wounds to heal before I can celebrate and be around these things with you. I will celebrate again with you someday; give me time to get there. Please don't tell me you want the "old me" back, because in reality now, I am not that person anymore. This isn't a bad thing—I've just been changed by a profound, life-altering experience. I'm not going down a bad path, just a new one. There are many things that will remain unchanged in me, but some will never be the same. This is okay. Accept the newness in me, and know that I'm still getting used to it too.

What can you do to help me? First, talk with me about my child. Very few people ever received the blessing of knowing him, but you did. So speak his name, remember his birthday, tell me what he meant to you. As his mother, I yearn for these things. Second, find ways to lovingly remember my baby and honor his life. Don't let his memory fade away. Third, let me cry and know it's not bad if I do. I have found there is no more effective way to deal with my heartbreak sometimes than to just cry. I feel better most times after I have cried. Tears flow easily from me since the death of my baby. I can't really control it most of the time. Don't attempt to try to stop it or apologize for making me cry. Crying is a good thing. It's going to be a part of who I am for a while. Let's just allow this and not get uncomfortable with it.

And finally, please know that I have never felt anything so painful, so deeply sad, so completely overwhelming, as what I am feeling right now. Every morning that I get up and go on with life without my baby is hard, and every day that I do is a victory for me. I ask you please just be with me as I try to find my way to do this. I know hope and joy will return to me. Grief is a difficult form of self-discovery—it's making me define things anew in my life. Please know in these weeks after my baby's death, I have learned how much more precious your love is to me than I ever realized it to be before. I value you in my life so very much and hope, through this honest sharing of my heartfelt thoughts, that our journey through this difficult time can be a little easier now.

With all my love,

COMMUNICATING WITH FAMILY AND FRIENDS

REFLECTIONS

FOR THE GRIEVING PARENT:
Write a letter to your family and friends to help improve your communication with them.

FOR THE FAMILY AND FRIENDS OF A GRIEVING PARENT:
Write a note to your loved one telling them how much the deceased baby meant to you and how he or she made a positive impact on your life.

The Wisdom of Angels

PART II

What's "Normal" Now?

Heather One of my friends recently told me, "I want my old friend back." I thought to myself, "That old friend is gone." What was normal for me before is not normal for me now. After eighteen months since Connor's death, I can look back and see that I have changed tremendously, but the core of me is still alive and well.

After Connor's death, I felt like a shell of my old self—a totally empty shell. I went about the mechanics of daily life, but found little joy in it. Over time, and with a lot of focus on being thankful for everything good in my life, that shell began to fill up again. Now I have what could be called a normal routine. I also can find joy again in my work, friends, and family. I wonder if my shell could have gotten so full without the birth of my second child, Hayden. I don't know really. Hayden's life is a tremendous joy to me. I know she is a big reason for me to feel alive and well again.

What has filled the shell of me is new and different. The core is still the same, but I have definitely expanded the definition of "me" and "normal" through this experience. Some of the new me is better, and maybe some is worse. For instance, I don't have my old unbridled positive attitude about life anymore. Because of Connor, I understand more about suffering in this world, and this led me to be much more empathetic than I ever used to be. So ultimately, maybe this change is a good thing. Other examples of the new me: I have a stronger relationship with God, I appreciate my loved ones more, I fill my life with more purposeful activity, I prioritize work and family and community outreach differently, I value friendships in new ways, I feel things more strongly, I am much more thankful for the little things.

I am different. My old self is gone. I filled my shell up differently. But I view myself as more normal now than I ever was before.

Allison What is normal? I feel now like I did my first summer home after freshman year of college. I came back to live in my old room and hang out with my old friends. This was all very familiar and automatic, but it didn't fit me anymore. I had grown, changed, and expanded my life experiences. My normal had changed, and I needed to find a new routine and purpose.

Now in the aftermath of Brennen's life and death, I'm looking for a new normal once again. Sure, I still go to work, do my chores, and have my lazy Saturdays after a hard week. These give outward signs that my life has returned to "normal." But my thoughts, prayers, dreams, hopes, and desires have changed. The inside of me is different. A year after my son's death, not having him here with me still makes me feel awkward with any of these routines. I had expected and planned for my life to change once Brennen arrived, but the fact is, things didn't change the way I wanted them to. All is not as it should be. I guess that uneasiness will be there until I find my new normal: without my dreams for Brennen. I need new dreams.

Linda Early into my grief, I used to be really concerned about "getting back to normal." I used to worry that I had lost myself, my personality, and my soul. Now I realize that I didn't lose these things as much as they have simply changed. I have accepted the fact that my old self and my old ways are gone. My normal has changed.

Normal for me used to be my very optimistic attitude about life. I am no longer that optimistic. No wonder younger people tend to be so much more optimistic and carefree than older people—they haven't seen enough of the hurts of this world to be otherwise. Madison's death has matured my thinking: I know bad things can and do happen.

Normal for me used to be my feelings of invincibility. I had my sense of security taken from me when my daughter died. I know I am vulnerable.

Normal for me used to be blind faith. I believed that if I prayed, God would answer my prayer the way I wanted. I don't believe that anymore. I pray now for God's will to be done, rather than requesting specific outcomes, because I know it is God's plan that prevails, not mine. I view prayer very differently now.

Normal for me used to be waking up every morning with very few concerns or problems. I now wake up every day feeling a hole in my heart that is buried with my daughter. After you experience the death of your baby, you don't "go back" to normal. There is no going back. You "move forward" into a new normal.

In our situation, we have to consider what the normal should be for Kaitlyn, Madison's twin sister. As she gets older, I find myself trying to make sure that we maintain a sense of normalcy for her. We keep on going for her, and in doing so we experience so much joy and love. Kaitlyn deserves to have a normal life—it should not be constantly disrupted by the grief her parents feel over her sister. Yes, Kaitlyn will know about her twin sister and our grief, but we plan to give her a childhood full of happiness so that she can be carefree as children should be. We'll make sure this is the "normal" Kaitlyn will always know.

Tania My new normal might be considered abnormal by others. I think it is normal to talk about Lanika, and others do not. When I sign a card, I put all three of my princesses' names on it because I have three princesses. Other people's minds do not think that way, and they think I am abnormal. Everyone believes I go through a normal day with typical routines, meals, and relationships, but at the end of the day, it was an abnormal day because my Lanika was not there. There is nothing normal about my Lanika not being there. So many people I know push to "get back to normal." I want to scream and say to them, "This is normal. The acting I am doing with you all is abnormal."

Audra I have learned that to suffer is actually to be normal—suffering is part of human existence. None of us are promised a rose garden throughout all of life. Those who have no disappointments or suffering in life are rare, and I believe they are the abnormal. They can't easily relate to the great majority of us who do experience great tribulations at various times in life.

WHAT'S "NORMAL" NOW?

REFLECTIONS

FOR THE GRIEVING PARENT:
How has your "normal" changed since the death of your baby? Have you become comfortable with your new normal yet?

FOR THE FAMILY AND FRIENDS OF A GRIEVING PARENT:
In what way do you see your loved one reestablishing themselves in a new normal? How are you supporting them in doing this?

Vicky What have I learned? When a parent experiences the death of their baby, some of their old ways die along with their child. The death of a baby is pivotal in a mother and father's life. The direction of their lives is irrevocably altered. There really is no option to go back to what they knew before as standard. Life moves forward, and grieving parents must search for a "new normal." The saving grace is that this new normal does not have to be negative. If they grieve in healthy ways, the death experience can expand a person's personality in many positive directions. The capacity for love and caring, for sorrow and joy, and for purpose and meaning can all deepen. The ability to understand another's pain can be heightened. The ability to love can be magnified. The motivation to seek higher purpose in the activities of life can be strengthened. The belief in God can be sharpened. These attributes can all become part of the "new normal." There are plenty of ways grieving parents can take the hard, cold lessons of death and grief and eventually steer their future (albeit different from what they ever wanted it to be) into a good and meaningful normal.

My Faith Has Been Tested

Heather Before losing Connor, I took my faith for granted. My life was good, and it was easy to be faithful. When challenged with the horrible reality that my son died, it was no longer easy for me to be faithful. After Connor died, I questioned everything concerning God.

When I was in the NICU, I prayed constantly. I believed that if I prayed with loving intentions and with a pure heart, surely God would answer my prayers. I prayed desperately for Connor to live. But my prayers were met with silence…frustrating and cold silence. I admit, I feel angry about this. I am a good person. Connor was completely innocent, and he suffered. How could God not answer my prayers? I can't imagine how taking a child from loving parents could be part of a good God's plan. I have come to realize, and I'm trying to accept, that I will never truly understand this until I join Connor in heaven. It's beyond my faith; it's beyond my understanding as long as I am merely of this world.

Immediately after losing Connor, I went through a "research phase"—I asked questions, read books, even decided to read my Bible from cover to cover, all in an attempt to find out who, what, and where God is. I felt like I didn't know God anymore, and that I needed to find God if I was to ever feel peace after the loss of my son. While I still cannot even begin to understand God, it was a good thing for me to do. What I have learned is that I'll be searching for answers all my life. This is what active faith is. I think my faith has matured because of this process, from a simplistic "grant me my wish" approach to a "help me understand your plan for me" approach.

I have also come to realize that God did not "do this to me" to punish me, although I have spent some sleepless nights questioning this. Was I too lazy in my faith? Did God do this to me to wake me up and teach me a lesson? Is this God's way of bringing me back to a more active faith? Why would an innocent child have to suffer for my sins? While I don't have any good answers about why God allowed this to happen, and I am angry about it, I am thankful for the lessons I've learned and the clarity I've obtained. For example, I know that God did not desert me during my darkest hour, but put people in my path to help. These people have tremendously enriched my life. What I need to discern is why my life has taken this path, and what can I do to make something good come of it.

I know my faith needs to continue maturing. Connor's death will ultimately enrich my faith rather than diminish it.

Tania We were created to live our lives focused on God. The loss of Lanika and grieving her has changed my focus on God. But all this did not change one heartbeat of my trust in God. I know even more now that I need to trust. Before Lanika, I had faith in me. I knew I was a good person, I was strong in my faith, I felt I could do anything. Now I realize this isn't true. I am not capable of everything, no matter how hard I try and no matter how hard I pray. Therefore, I need to have trust and faith in God who is stronger than me. It's my only way through this life. It's my only way to heaven. It's my only way to Lanika.

Audra Since Gabe came and went in my life, I have adjusted the way I pray. I used to pray for things and certain outcomes. Now I pray for the wisdom to cope with God's plan. While I admit I have found it hard to believe that God is good while I experience so much bad, I still have strong faith.

Allison Since my son Brennen died, my faith has been on a rollercoaster just as much as my feelings and emotions have been. I have had days of extreme anger and frustration with God. I have had days of heartfelt thanksgiving and joy. I have had days of doubt and confusion. I have had days of clarity and peace. There is no complacent middle ground for my faith anymore. Before Brennen, I "coasted" in my faith in God; now I can no longer do that.

I grew up in the Church. My dad is a minister and I have always been taught to go to God. "Give God your burdens." "Prayer works miracles." "If God brings you to it, God will bring you through it." These are things I had been taught and things I thought I believed in. But that was before Brennen. When Brennen died, none of it made sense to me anymore. I truly felt forgotten and forsaken. I questioned my faith. I was angry at God and found it hard to deal with that anger until a wise person told me one day that anger is okay. In order to be in a real relationship with someone, even God, we do disagree and arrive at points of anger. It's the sign of an engaged relationship. Anger at God is okay…for a while.

Since Brennen's death, I feel the need to be closer to God and to live my faith more actively. My thoughts, feelings, and expectations of God have all changed dramatically. While I don't believe that God wants to see any of us suffer, we are not promised a life free of suffering. From God comes the courage, strength, and character it takes to endure these difficult times. God has given me courage and strength, and I am thankful for it. I have felt God loving me through this. As I am rebuilding myself and my faith, I am finding my peace with God. I know that, in the end, the closer that I am to God, the closer I am to my son.

Linda My husband and I were both raised in strong Christian homes. Our parents were ministers, and looking back, it seems that if the church doors were open, we were there. We were raised to trust the Lord at all times. We were raised to believe that prayer can change everything, and that the Lord has a plan for everyone's life.

On the night we were told to rush to the hospital because the doctors did not think Madison would survive the night, our first response was to pray. Walking to the car, on the way to the hospital, all the way to the NICU, we prayed. Our family gathered in the NICU break room, held hands, bowed our heads, and prayed together for her survival. I truly believed God would answer our prayers and Madison would survive. I knew God was capable of miracles: Madison would be healed. I never imagined the horrors I would be dealing with later that night. I didn't understand why God did not answer our prayers to save Madison. I was in complete shock, and I didn't know what to feel or think.

In the days to come, we had to make a deliberate choice to trust in the Lord, and to trust that this was God's plan for our lives. We did not like the plan at all, but we had to believe that God knew better than we did. This was very hard to do, and it still is. But I choose to believe there are reasons for all this beyond what I can ever comprehend. I now believe that God did answer our prayers to heal Madison. It was just that God chose to heal her in heaven, not here on earth with us.

I would say our faith has grown stronger since we lost our daughter. We have rededicated our lives to the Lord and have chosen to live our lives in a way that would honor Madison's memory. We are raising Kaitlyn to know and love God.

MY FAITH HAS BEEN TESTED

REFLECTIONS

FOR THE GRIEVING PARENT:
Has the death of your baby tested your faith? If yes, in what ways? What have you learned so far? Do you pray differently now than before?

FOR THE FAMILY AND FRIENDS OF A GRIEVING PARENT:
In what ways do you see your loved one struggling with their faith in this time of grief? If they are questioning God, how can you help them find answers? How might you help them lean on their faith instead of turn from it right now?

Vicky Being witness to so much suffering and death during my nursing career has tested my faith much like these women describe. Coming to know these five women in particular, their families, and their painful grief, makes me all the more hungry for the answers to the question posed in all instances of infant death: Why? I have scoured books, asked nuns and priests, and listened intently to funeral sermons for the answers. Why did this baby have to suffer and die? Why do these good parents have to endure the terrible suffering of their loss? In the end, I suppose the best explanation I have ever heard is that we are not meant for this world. This world is not "it" for us. There is something beyond this life, and it is better. If we believe this world is "it," then death would leave us all hopeless. If Gabriel only battled necrotizing enterocolitis to die, if Connor only lived twenty days to merely suffer, if Madison left behind a twin sister only to die, if Lanika died only to break her parents' and sister's hearts, and if Brennen only lived to bring his parents a lifetime of sorrow, then how utterly hopeless, meaningless, and void of any joy our lives would be. I cannot believe this would be our loving Creator's plan. I do not believe God created us to be hopeless, joyless souls. I believe we pass through this earthly world, tested and battered, to go on to something more divine. The trials are temporary on earth, and the reward is forever in heaven. Yes: Gabriel, Connor, Madison, Lanika, and Brennen passed through this world all too briefly, and those who loved these babies will mourn their loss for the remainder of their earthly lives. But this earthly time is not "it." I believe there is more. And this is what gives me a deep faith in a loving God. In the face of death, this is what gives me hope.

What Is the Purpose of Suffering?

Tania I question why I need to go through the suffering I'm experiencing in my grief. I know my suffering will be easier to bear when I begin to really understand its purpose. I ask: "Why is any of the suffering I see in the world allowed?" I am praying to Allah to help me answer this question so I can find my peace. I am finding the answers, but they come very slowly.

My suffering makes me react differently now to life than I did before. Before, I didn't know how many broken pieces a person can become. I didn't know how much someone can bleed inside. I didn't know it was possible to not be able to distinguish between days and nights. Now when I see someone else suffering, I can actually feel their pain. My insides cry with them. I find I can communicate with them, sometimes not with words, but just with eyes. Also, now I respect life so much more than I ever did before. I cherish life. I cherish my two surviving daughters, husband, and family so much more. Is this what Allah wants of me—to communicate better with people and cherish life more?

I believe that suffering makes us know life and people better. Suffering makes us live more honestly. It has done this for me, and I find peace in this.

Heather Since Connor's death, it seems as if blinders have been taken off my eyes. I notice suffering in the world all around me much more than I ever did before. Turn on the news or look around. Starvation, sickness, genocide, war, drug addiction, abandonment, job loss, bullying—suffering is everywhere. I was aware of these things before; the difference now is I feel it. Before, I was detached from the world's suffering and, in all honesty, I reacted very little to it. Now I'm in the middle of suffering. I know it. I feel it—not just my own suffering, but the suffering of others as well. I think my suffering has developed a new personality trait in me: I feel drawn to do whatever I can to alleviate the suffering of others. No one's suffering should be invisible. No one should suffer alone. I see suffering with crystal-clear vision, and I react now with much greater empathy and understanding than I ever did before. I am more humble about it.

I know that I have learned the virtues of empathy, understanding, and humility through my suffering. I'm appreciative of what I have and take little for granted. I am a better person for it. But this seems to me an almost cruel form of education. Is there no other way? Is the purpose of suffering to teach us true understanding, empathy and humility? Would I have learned these virtues any other way besides my suffering? I wonder…

Linda I wonder a lot why my daughters had to suffer as they did. Why do Brendan and I have to suffer through this grief now? There are no easy answers.

I am looking for and finding my answers to the purpose of suffering by making my life more purposeful. I have become an active volunteer with our hospital's NICU parent support group. I try to help other parents who are struggling through the terrifying NICU experience, and I draw comfort from the fact that

Madison's life is having a positive effect beyond my own family. Is the purpose of my suffering to learn how to lessen the suffering of others? I don't know, but I think the answer lies somewhere in this process. And there is something peaceful in finding the answers there.

If I had a choice, I would have chosen to live the remainder of my life with two healthy twin daughters. I wanted that so badly. I still want it. I wasn't given the choice to suffer or not. No one gets that choice. Suffering comes to us all at some time or another, and it is not welcome any time. I don't know the answers yet as to the purpose of suffering. But I do know that as a result of my suffering, I live a more purposeful life. And this makes me a better person than I may have been before I knew suffering. I think this Scripture verse speaks to this very thing:

Blessed be the God and Father of our Lord Jesus Christ, the Father of mercies and the God of all consolation, who consoles us in all our affliction, so that we may be able to console those who are in any affliction with the consolation with which we ourselves are consoled by God.

2 Corinthians 1:3-4

Audra I believe suffering to be a medium for learning compassion. It allows an opportunity for self-improvement. Suffering is something like coming down with the flu. It is miserable to go through, but getting through it builds up certain immunities in you. The next time you suffer, you have more internal strength to survive. You have built up knowledge and a power that is useful to you next time. Yes, suffering is hard, but it is not necessarily all bad. I would rather have suffered what I have suffered than to never have had Gabriel in my life.

Allison As a teacher, I have for many years taught a unit covering *The Diary of Anne Frank*. Before Brennen came and went from my life, I thought this a good, interesting book. But even having read it several times, the book never really moved me. This year, as I read the account with my students of this dear young woman's suffering, her family's suffering, the Jewish people's suffering during the Holocaust, I found myself becoming extremely emotional and crying over it. My suffering transformed me into a student in my own classroom this year. I had learned (for the first time really) to be truly compassionate. Before, I did not fully understand other people's suffering. Now I know suffering. Now I feel it. The suffering of others doesn't just pass by me unnoticed anymore. I see their suffering, I feel their suffering, and I am moved to do something about it.

I do not believe suffering is a punishment; it is a call to action. Suffering can be a window into deeper goodness and more compassionate love.

WHAT IS THE PURPOSE OF SUFFERING?

REFLECTIONS

FOR THE GRIEVING PARENT:
Since you began your grief journey, have you questioned why you have to suffer? What answers have you found? How do you think your suffering has changed you?

FOR THE FAMILY AND FRIENDS OF A GRIEVING PARENT:
What do you think the purpose of suffering is? Have you seen your loved one changed by having to endure this suffering? In what ways? Have you had a discussion with your loved one about the purpose of suffering? If yes, which of these has been your approach?

(1) To ask your loved one, "Tell me more why you think that."

(2) To tell your loved one, "Let me tell you what I think the purpose of suffering is."

Which do you think may be the more helpful approach?

Vicky Suffering does in fact have great purpose in our lives. I believe it is one means of obtaining grace. If you are a student of history, or if you examine the lives of the Good Grief Group women, there is a recurrent pattern. Many people, after enduring deep personal suffering, go on to do very wonderful things. Abraham Lincoln, Corrie Ten Boom, St. Maximillian Kolbe, Theodore Roosevelt, Elie Wiesel, Helen Keller, Pope John Paul II, Gandhi, and Nelson Mandela quickly come to mind as cases in point. Perhaps one of our contemporaries, who saw more suffering than most, was Mother Teresa of Calcutta. What did she learn from the suffering she saw in the impoverished streets where she worked so tirelessly for forty years? Mother Theresa often wrote and spoke about seeing the face of God in the very faces of the suffering people she cared for. She taught that God is revealed most clearly to us in our suffering. God is a God of love, and we are taught to love God and all humanity more deeply. While it is certainly not the method any of us would ever willingly choose to better ourselves, suffering does seem to have a loving purpose. And I believe we've been left a great example to help us as we endure our own personal suffering. Suffering afflicted Jesus—even he was not immune from it. He, like us, did not welcome it and asked for it to be taken from him. There is comfort in knowing this. And so I wonder, is suffering the greatest lesson of all about love? Is it God's way to form us into the deeply compassionate, loving human beings—the "saints" —we never could have become on our own?

THEME 15

Can I Ever Hope Again?

Allison Is there any other time in life when you're more hopeful than during pregnancy? During my pregnancy with Brennen I carried so much hope for what his addition to our family would bring. When things started to go bad, and I spent all those weeks on bed rest, I still kept a very cheerful attitude and hoped we would make it through this rocky journey. When he was born and struggled so much for every breath, we hoped for the miracle he so desperately needed to survive. And on the night Brennen died, I felt that all of my hopes burst like a huge bubble.

Hope carried me through the scariest experience of my life. Death and grief stripped me of that hope. My glass was no longer half full or half empty—it was shattered. The idea of investing in hope again was not only terrifying, it was absurd.

As I have worked to rebuild my life, I have learned that it is impossible to build a life worth living without hope. Almost by accident, and against my "self-preservation" desires, I caught myself slowly hoping for the future again. I actually couldn't help it. It must be human nature, or at least my nature, to hope. I desperately want to believe that good guys always win, that there's light at the end of the tunnel, that every cloud has a silver lining. While I exercised great caution, even stubbornness, in allowing it to come back into my life, I did experience hope again. And I know this is a great blessing. Finding hope helps me move forward and carry my grief.

My reality has taught me that despite the fact that the good guy does NOT always win, hope is possible. The apostle Paul tells us: "And now faith, hope, and love abide, these three; and the greatest of these is love" (1 Corinthians 13:13). This is my motto in life now. Hope abides in me.

Audra Yes, it is true that immediately after terrible life experiences you find yourself incapable of hoping for good things again. All of a sudden, it's no longer in you to do so. It's a defense mechanism—you avoid hope because you don't want to be hurt again. But what would life be like if we allowed ourselves to stay in such a state? How empty and aimless our lives would be if we didn't hope for a brighter, better future. I choose not to have that kind of life. Therefore, while it scares me to do so, I have broken through my fear and I have, very slowly, become a hopeful person again.

Heather Four months after Connor's death, I became pregnant again. To dare to hope like this was the scariest thing I have ever done. My second pregnancy was an emotionally and excruciatingly difficult nine months for me. At times, I wondered if I would lose my mind worrying for my second child's future. How could I dare to be hopeful for her when I knew the painful reality of what had happened, despite my best efforts, to Connor? Even one year after Hayden's healthy, happy arrival into my life, I still find myself afraid to hope for her future. At those times, I fear losing a future with her, and that my hopes and dreams for my second child will be dashed like they were for my first child. Nothing has ever indicated to me that this would happen, but it still is a fear that creeps occasionally into my mind.

I am definitely learning to hope again, but with caution. I don't ever want to experience this type of hurt and grief again, so I guess my caution is my way to protect myself. I started by hoping for fairly inconsequential happenings—those types of things that held little risk. Then I moved on to bigger things. Over time, I've come to realize that most things I hope for pale in comparison in how I hope for my children. There is incredible hope wrapped up in a mother's love for her children. I don't waste my energy in hoping for inconsequential things for Hayden. I just want her to live in good health and be happy. Hayden does not have to be the best, brightest, tallest, prettiest...she just has to be. This is my greatest hope.

Tania In the first months after Lanika left us, I was scared to do just about anything, but I was especially scared to hope. I didn't want to risk putting more pain on top of what I already felt. I knew I couldn't take any more pain. But you cannot live like that unless you stay in bed and go nowhere. I had my lovely husband and two daughters still, and our family started to hope again. Life keeps going and hope goes with it. On Lanika's first birthday, I found out that I was pregnant again. I laughed and cried at that time—I was so happy thinking about a new life to add to our family and so scared to hope like this again. But the happiness ruled over my fear. Only a short time later, however, on the one-year anniversary of Lanika's death, I lost that pregnancy. The life of Lanika outside me was the same as the life of this baby inside me. All I could do was ask, "Why?" The pain is still so much. I am very scared to ever hope again. But I am human, I like to dream, and it makes me happy to hope for good things and look for a sunny day again. I will hope again, when my pain has healed.

Linda A single sentence from the doctor snuffed my hopeful, optimistic self: "There is nothing we can do." After her death, I found it hard to hope for anything again. However, I had the blessing of another child to love and become absorbed in. I think Kaitlyn certainly helped me find a way to hope again, and I am very thankful for this.

I have very cautiously allowed hope to reenter my mind and my heart. It scares me to do so, but I want to. I have a daughter, a husband, and a family counting on me. What kind of life would we have if we didn't hope for good things to come, or dream what will be? I have so many hopes and dreams for Kaitlyn, and I want to enjoy them with her. In order to go on living, and live well, I know I must let hope back in. I don't want to live a hope-less existence. Madison would not have wanted that for us. Kaitlyn is showing us the way back to hopefulness.

We talked about suffering and its purpose. I believe when you come out on the other side of suffering, you find a new way to hope. The Apostle Paul beautifully wrote of this progression:

> *And not only that, but we also boast in our sufferings, knowing that suffering produces endurance, and endurance produces character, and character produces hope.*
> *Romans 5: 3-4*

CAN I EVER HOPE AGAIN?

REFLECTIONS

FOR THE GRIEVING PARENT:
Have you found yourself scared to hope for anything good in your future? If yes, how have you tried to allow yourself to hope again? How scary is this for you to do right now? What is your biggest fear? What is your biggest hope?

FOR THE FAMILY AND FRIENDS OF A GRIEVING PARENT:
Can you see why your loved one might find it extremely difficult to think about ever hoping again? Have you sat down with them and asked the question, "What are your biggest fears in life right now?" Did you have a listening, non-judgmental approach or did you try to fix their fears?

Vicky From my observations, I have surmised that one of the darkest moments in the early stages of profound grief is when the griever finds life void of any hope. And without hope, what is the use of getting out of bed in the morning, or of expending energy on anything? A hopeless life leads quickly to despair, absence of desire, inactivity, isolation, and nothingness. Living hopelessly is no way to live. Grieving people come to know this when they realize it is better to live with the chance of hurt than to not live in hope. Despite these women's cautious, understandable, sometimes defiant attitude toward letting hope back into their lives again, hope came back to them anyways. Isn't it remarkable that, like Allison said, it couldn't be helped but to let hope back in? Look around: Hope constantly surrounds us. There is hope in a farmer planting his crops. There is hope as newlyweds walk down the aisle. There is hope when a new store opens down the street. There is hope in a caterpillar. There is hope in the rosebud just before it is ready to bloom. There is hope in the dawn. When life seems hopeless, look around with fresh, open eyes, and see how hope is expressed and realized in myriad ways. Finding hope again—slowly, cautiously—is surely a way for grievers to move forward in their journey toward peace.

I Fear Life More and Death Less

Tania I have seen several deaths. I was there with my father when he died, my mother when she left us, and Lanika when she died. Death is not unknown to me. I don't believe I fear death, because I don't believe it's a bad thing for the person who is dying. (It's bad for those left behind, because we hurt and miss them so much.) I fear when death will happen to my loved ones. I wasn't ready to lose my father, mother, or Lanika. I suppose no one is ever ready to see the loves of their lives go on to heaven. Fear of death can increase our fear of life. I know that all life eventually ends, but I don't want it to end earlier than it has to. I just want all my loved ones to stay safe. I can only trust in Allah and pray for safety.

Heather Because of Connor, my views of life and death have dramatically changed. The realities of both collided in those twenty days that Connor was with us. Even though I had lived thirty-three years prior to my son's birth, I became much wiser about life in his twenty days. What did I learn? Life is hard. Life is not fair. Bad things happen to good people. People who suffer don't deserve to suffer. And people who have good fortune don't necessarily deserve their good fortune. Those who are greatly blessed in life most often do not have any idea just how blessed they are. People who are most precious to me can and will die someday. None of us are assured of tomorrow. These are the hard lessons of life. Having learned these things, I fear what may come in life more than I ever did before. However, I also learned that good people will surround me when I am faced with frightening things in life, and that I don't have to bear my fears alone. I find great comfort in knowing this, and so my fear does not paralyze me. I have learned the lovely fact that there are many people out there doing good, helping others through suffering.

My son suffered. His suffering finally came to an end when he was put into our arms to be loved into heaven. His suffering ended then, and so his best day was also his last day of living.

There were times after Connor's death when I thought I could not wait to feel the relief from pain that comes with death. Connor experienced only pain and suffering in his life, and death was his relief from his world of suffering. While I want to go on living a long, fulfilling life, I see much less reason to fear death now. When my own final day comes, when I am on my death bed, after I have done everything I want to do, I just may see that as the best day of my life too.

Audra Gabriel's death was not the first loss of a close loved one I have experienced. My dad died when I was eight. I learned early that life is hard and there will be difficulties to get through. Before Gabe, I had already learned that bad things sometimes happen to us despite our best efforts to make it otherwise. So I wouldn't say this experience of Gabriel's life and death has made me fear life any more than I did before. I can't say that I'm really scared of life. I just understand that it won't always be rosy.

My experience with Gabriel didn't change my outlook on death either. Losing my dad at such an early age made me ponder death and begin to examine it a long time ago. I've always had some fear of death because of the unknowns about it. I like to know for certain how things are going to be. But death is that "great unknown." People have some strong ideas about it, but no one can say with absolute certainty what happens to us after death. I believe in heaven and I believe a better place awaits us when we die, but not knowing the details, not knowing for certain, has always made me a little fearful of death.

Allison I don't know if I was ever really "afraid" of death. I was more afraid of the unknown that death represents. Death is no longer an unknown to me. I know it now. I know that in death I will not have to bear pain and sadness any longer. I know that in death I will be able to fill my aching arms with my beautiful son and kiss him tenderly.

While death became clearer to me because of Brennen, life suddenly became more of an unknown. His death shook my understanding of life. I didn't know how to define myself anymore, how to overcome this sadness, how to handle the new emotions that threatened to overwhelm me. I was scared of what lay ahead of me. I have learned, with the help of many loving people and the return of hope, that it is possible to live with and overcome these fears.

So yes, after Brennen, I fear the difficulties of life more and the unknown of death less. I am by no means done living. I have so many plans, so much to experience yet. I live a more real life now, a more purposeful life, a more aware life than I ever did before. My life is good, and I plan to live it with gusto. I just know now that the beauty of what awaits me through my own death, whenever it may come, is something to look forward to and not fear.

Linda Living after Madison died was hard. After her death, I could not face talking to anyone outside my immediate family. I could not talk to anyone openly about her except to my husband. After a few weeks, I summoned the nerve to call a few friends, but talking to them for the first time was extremely difficult. What do you talk about? Brendan and I couldn't go back to our house for two weeks after Madison died because we couldn't face entering the house we knew she'd never come home to. A friend delivered food to us on the day of her funeral, and I hid in the bathroom because I couldn't face seeing a friend, seeing anyone, yet. After about a month, I tried to visit my office. I felt like throwing up as I walked in the doors to face everyone. I couldn't wait to get out of there. You must know this is all highly uncharacteristic of me. Death changed what I knew about life. Experiencing my daughter's death made living harder for me. But on the other hand, experiencing the life of my other daughter gave me reason to enjoy life again. She gave me reason to smile, laugh, and hope again. Do I still fear life without Madison? Of course, but now I have a reason to enjoy life as well.

Because Madison has changed my view of life so much, it is only natural that it has changed my view of death as well. I probably still fear my own death, but less now because I know someone is waiting for me. If heaven really is a perfect place where we will live in eternal happiness, then Madison has got to be part of that eternal happiness for me. When I think of heaven now, I envision Madison in the loving arms of Jesus and being sung lullabies by the angels. I envision myself holding her again, and never ever having to let her go. With these visions, I could never fear the afterlife anymore. How can I fear it? My daughter waits there for me.

I FEAR LIFE MORE AND DEATH LESS

REFLECTIONS

FOR THE GRIEVING PARENT:
Do you have new fears about living now? If yes, describe them and how you deal with them. Have your thoughts about death changed since you experienced your child's death? In what ways?

FOR THE FAMILY AND FRIENDS OF A GRIEVING PARENT:
In what ways have you seen your loved one's outlook on life and death change since their baby died? Are you comfortable talking about the topic of death with your loved one? If not, why not? Have you explored with them any of their new hopes and fears about life and death?

Vicky I have been with each one of these women in some of their moments of great fear and wondered, "How will they ever overcome this? How will they conquer the overwhelming fear they experience?" I wanted so much to erase all their fears, and to tell them, "Everything will be okay." But I could not honestly speak these words to any of them, and I didn't. I honestly did not know if, in fact, everything would eventually be okay for them. All I could do was try to be with them, and let them know they did not have to face their fears alone. In so doing, I have been witness to a truly admirable display of steely courage. It took great courage for Linda to go back to work, for Heather to pick up her son's ashes from the funeral home, for Allison to take down her son's crib, for Tania to donate all her stored-up breast milk to a milk bank, for Audra to hold her son alone as he died. Can you just imagine what it took for them to do these things? As they all battled fears, these grieving mothers demonstrated uncommon valor, and I greatly respect each one of them for it. They did not allow their fears to paralyze them from going on. Audra, Heather, Linda, Tania, and Allison each live more aware of the harsh realities of life, but they have summoned up remarkable courage to live fully, despite these realities. They did not run away from their fears: They faced them. They have taught me that it takes tremendous courage to journey through grief, and I stand in admiration of them.

Death and Grief as Teachers

Allison Without a doubt, I have learned much through my son's life and death, and my grief over his loss. Some of the lessons I have learned:

- How to love—what love is
- How to let go when I need to—I am not in control.
- How to believe—in the will of God, in the support that surrounds you, in the hope that's always there
- How to survive—I know now even the worst of times do get better. It is within me to withstand and overcome.

These are "forced" wisdoms. I gained them unwillingly. As a teacher by profession, I can see I have been a stubborn pupil. Why did I never see and understand these things before? I have been just like my junior high students, who ask me daily, "Why do we need to know this? Why is this so important?" I fought these lessons which were forced upon me.

With this new knowledge, I can say my life has blossomed. My senses have become awakened, and my heart feels and knows true, pure, perfect love like it never did before. I have found new purpose and direction. My ideas of family and basic life values have grown dramatically stronger. I have become more resolved to focus on what is truly important in life.

I find great comfort in knowing that my son's life and death have taught me so much. There is a pervasive sense of peace and hope that comes to me when I realize Brennen's time on this earth will continue to guide me and teach me about my own life. He goes on because his lessons go on.

Linda   I have learned many positive lessons through my daughter's life and death, and my grief over her loss.

- **I can endure much more** than I ever thought I could. I have learned that I am a stronger person than I ever imagined myself to be.
- **My husband is even more amazing** than I ever knew him to be before. He is and has been a wonderful father to both our girls. It is true: A new side of your partner is revealed once they become a parent.
- **Faith brings one through difficult times.** Both my husband and I really leaned on the faith we gained in our childhood to help bring us through this tragedy.
- **People will surprise you** greatly and support you through your dark times in ways you could never imagine. People I never expected have reached out to me, and they have been the strongest supports to me throughout this tragedy. God brought them to me; I was not left to carry this heavy burden alone. I have learned a great deal about the most unlikely sources of love and support, and this has brought me an enduring sense of peace.

Tania   At first, I did not notice, but I can see now that Lanika's life and death were learning experiences for me. I've come to know a person's true strength is often hidden until it's most needed. At first, I did not think I had the strength to get through this. I have learned now that I do. I've also learned that Allah does not give us everything we ask for. Our lives go according to Allah's plans; we humans do not control everything. When we understand this, life is easier in our families, marriages, work, and friendships. And lastly, I've learned that letting go is part of holding on to the ones you love. It is one of the hardest parts about loving. But if you make the most of every moment you have with your loved ones, you will come to know that as hard as the letting go is, the loving makes it all worth it. This is what I have learned. Other grieving parents may learn similar lessons, or they may learn altogether new ones. I say trust yourself, listen closely to your heart, and you will find your path and wisdom.

Heather Loss and grief were not just "a short disruption" to my life. Death and grief had transformative lessons for me. I hope I am a wiser, better person because of the learning that has taken place in my life because of Connor. What sort of things have I learned?

- Motherhood is not to be taken for granted. It is a blessing given to us by the grace of God. Each of our children are gifts to us, no matter how long we have them, and it is a great privilege to be trusted with their lives while they are with us.

- The human spirit is eternally resilient. Me, my husband, the women writing this book with me—we have all learned that joy in living is possible again after a crushing, devastating loss. We have all surpassed just surviving: We have found beautiful ways to go on loving deeply.

- We all need to reprioritize. Work deadlines, car repairs, the new shoes I was saving to buy—all that became secondary to love and family during the twenty days of Connor's life, and I have no regrets about any of it. While I was pregnant with Hayden, my new priorities were re-emphasized. Now, as my life returns to a new normal, I hope I will carry this lesson forward and continue living with these priorities, and my future will be more honest and rewarding because of it.

- There are angels walking this earth. The nurses and doctors at the NICU are just one example of people who sacrifice so much of themselves to ease the suffering of others and to make the world a better place. These uncommonly compassionate professionals return day after day to engage in that epic struggle, forced to absorb the heartbreaks that come, while continuing always to strive for success. Their actions and words of understanding carry such value to me now. There are the angels who are well-known and famous, but we have angels in our own lives—truly good people who toil for others without reward.

I am grateful for the lessons death and grief have taught me. As the intensity of my grief continues to wane, I hope these lessons will remain forever strong in me. Learning these lessons has brought me peace and comfort.

Audra I feel I am a wiser person because of my experience of loss and grief. Through Gabriel's life and death, I have learned:

- to cherish the simplest pleasures of life, for often they're the greatest
- to not waste time or energy on unimportant matters
- to prioritize things in life better
- to be much less materialistic
- to be much more compassionate
- to be more patient

I have learned that the quality of my life depends on what I make of it. Days pass quickly, opportunities pass quickly, people pass quickly—so there should be no delay. I make the most of every day.

DEATH AND GRIEF AS TEACHERS

REFLECTIONS

FOR THE GRIEVING PARENT:
What lessons have you learned through your experience of death and grief? Which lesson(s) do you think will make the most significant impact on your life? Why?

FOR THE FAMILY AND FRIENDS OF A GRIEVING PARENT:
What life lessons have you learned from your experience with the loss of this baby? Have these lessons changed you in any way? If yes, in what specific ways? Have you shared a conversation with your loved one that explored the lessons they've learned in their grief journey and the lessons you've learned in yours?

Vicky Words often used in discussions concerning death and grief have a "compressive" nature to them. "Crushed," "broken," "pressed upon," "burdened down," "oppressed," "downtrodden," and "trampled" are but a few examples. While all these words have very appropriate places in such discussion, especially in the early months of grief, I have learned that they are inadequate when considering loss and grief in total. I believe, given time and healing, something opposite of "compression" can occur in grief. Something "expansive" is possible as well. This growth comes from lessons learned. I agree with Oliver Wendell Holmes when he wrote: "One's mind, once stretched by a new idea, never regains its original dimension." Knowledge expands. It widens one's universe. It increases abilities. It sharpens purpose. It does not allow you to revert back to being an unaware person. I have watched these women be "compressed" initially after their babies died, and I have also watched these grieving mothers gradually "expand" through their experience. Wisdom, born of loss and suffering, has left them with gifts they will benefit from for the rest of their lives. They have been stretched. Their children, families, friends, and coworkers will also benefit from their new-found knowledge. The ripple effect can only be imagined at this point. It is good to know it's not all been about compression. There has been expansion in Audra, Heather, Linda, Tania, and Allison's journeys toward peace.

THEME 18

Finding Consolation...
in Bits and Pieces

Allison Consolation is elusive and unpredictable in the aftermath of losing a baby. Where do you go, to whom do you turn when the world is upside down? I'm still searching. I have days where the pain of grief is so bad that I cannot find comfort in anything. So many things make me hurt, and sad, and long for Brennen. And then there are other days with wonderful moments, often when I have least expected them, in which I have found a peaceful comfort. Many of those moments have come from dragonflies.

When Vicky was Brennen's nurse, she created a special name card for his NICU bed that was decorated with stickers of dragonflies. In our initial conversation, Vicky discussed with us her reluctance to use dragonflies, but we all decided how lovely and appropriate they were. Incredibly, since the time of Brennen's death, dragonflies started coming to us when we needed comfort most—not every time, but enough so that I know it was not just coincidence. On my first Mother's Day following Brennen's death, Brian and I drove to a nearby park. It was one of those "aching empty-arms" kind of days, and both Brian and I were missing Brennen terribly. As we sat on our picnic blanket, the dragonflies unexpectedly flew all around us, and "posed" quite nicely for us to photograph some really beautiful pictures of them. Some of the hurt I was feeling that day seemed lifted from my shoulders as I enjoyed the dragonflies in that peaceful garden.

At least twice more dragonflies have come to me when I needed consolation. Once as I drove down the street crying during a particularly hard day, I heard an odd tapping on my car window. I looked up to see a dragonfly that kept flying into my window, as if to get my attention and make me take notice of it. Another time, Brian came home from a friend's child's birthday party feeling especially sad and missing Brennen. We spent half the night talking about and remembering Brennen, and I was very drained the next morning. As I went to the front porch to water our plants, a dragonfly landed on my watering can. I sat there next to the watering can for a while, and the dragonfly remained for a good while as well.

It seems that whenever my life becomes difficult, dragonflies are there to help lift me up. I see them now every morning on my walks, or in the evenings when I work in the yard. I can't thank Vicky enough for the beautiful gift of consoling remembrance she gave me. I always think serenely of Brennen whenever a dragonfly crosses my path. This brings me happiness and hope!

Linda Finding consolation is very hard for me. I find some of my greatest consolation in the presence of other mothers who have lost their children. Even though we lead different lives, we really understand each other and are bonded on a level like no other. Gathering with this Good Grief Group on a regular basis, and doing volunteer work together, has helped me immensely.

I also find consolation in my faith. The belief that I will be with Madison again some day is a beautiful, peaceful thought to me. Knowing she is at perfect peace with no pain or suffering is a consolation to me as well.

And lastly, I find great consolation in the arms of my husband, because I know he hurts just as much as I do. His pain, like mine, will never truly go away, and it is a comfort to find his knowing, loving embrace when I need help with the pain.

Heather I've learned that it takes a lot of searching, energy, and time to find effective consolation for my grief. It's a dynamic process. What comforted me last week doesn't necessarily comfort me this week. And what "works" varies greatly among grieving people. The things I did to try to find consolation included reading books and talking to people who would truly listen to me in a non-judgmental way when I talked about my grief. I prayed, I journaled, I went to a professional grief counselor, I accepted the grief outreach ministers from my church, I built a memory garden with Cole for Connor in our back yard, I became an active March of Dimes volunteer, I exercised, I got my mind back into my work, and I searched for answers to the big questions—what's the meaning of life, who is God, what is love. All of what I did, in varying degrees, did bring me some measure of consolation.

I would recommend to anyone who has lost a baby and is going through this terrible grief to be patient with the process and themselves. It takes time. Don't be afraid to look for consolation, and be willing to try new things if you think there's a chance that they might help. Actively search for a healthy means of recovering in all ways possible, because everyone is so different.

Audra My need to find consolation has changed over time. If you asked me this question eighteen months ago right after Gabriel died, my answer would have been completely different. I spent much energy desperately searching for something, anything that would give me consolation, and I did find some in a few people and things. Now my heart has a more contemplative view of its need for consolation, and I don't feel such a strong need to search for it any longer. It was okay for me to love my son, was it not? If I didn't love him, I wouldn't hurt like this. So it really is okay for me to hurt, is it not? For eighteen months I have been learning to live with the hurt. It does not overwhelm me so much anymore. I wonder then, do I really need to be consoled any longer?

Tania When Lanika first died, I felt like I was desperately searching for something, but I didn't know what to look for. Now I know I was seeking consolation. It came to me in small things. The staff at the hospital that made me feel proud to be Lanika's mother. In my Muslim faith, we have customs about cleaning the body before burial. I chose to bathe my lovely Lanika this last time. When I cleaned her, she looked like a princess. I dressed her with the "kafon," white pieces of cloth, and she looked like an angel. That brought me a lovely memory that consoles me to this day. When I donated all my breast milk to a milk bank, I felt my spirit rise up again. I could not wait to give it to them, knowing Lanika's milk would help many other babies. We had prayers set up on the fourth day after her death, and more than 150 people showed up at our house that night to pray with us for her. That meant the world to me. So many people came around, and just knowing they cared gave me great comfort.

And then I began meeting with Allison, Audra, Linda, Heather, and Vicky—we are all so different, and yet so much the same. By sharing our tears and laughter together, I have learned to breathe again. They've loved me, I've loved them, and it will go on for a lifetime because our babies have forever touched us all. I cannot begin to even think how I would have survived this without them—this Good Grief Group has very much consoled me. Our words to each other have been like priceless medicine. As time has gone on, I have found other things too—going to Lanika's grave, sometimes by myself, sometimes with my family, consoles me. Volunteering to help babies be born healthy through the March of Dimes helps my broken heart. Volunteering to help NICU families at the hospital gives me mental consolation. My faith helps me immensely—I read the Qur'an, help feed the poor and orphans of my old country, and we donate money to the mosque. I would tell any newly grieving parent—search, keep searching for those small things that help your spirit. You will find them here and there. Nothing will make all your pain and emptiness go away, but you will learn to breathe again.

FINDING CONSOLATION...IN BITS AND PIECES

REFLECTIONS

FOR THE GRIEVING PARENT:
Where have you searched for consolation? Have you found any? If yes, where or how? List instances you've had of being comforted. Do you see any patterns that have emerged?

FOR THE FAMILY AND FRIENDS OF A GRIEVING PARENT:
Knowing now how important it is for grievers to know their child is remembered, how can you show your loved one you remember their baby? When do you think are the most important times for you to do this? In what special, lasting ways can you show your loved one their baby mattered very much to you?

Vicky Grieving after the loss of a baby is harder—much harder—than I ever imagined. A year and a half into these women's grief journey, we came to discuss "Finding Consolation." I was particularly anxious to probe this theme with them, because it was getting to the crux of one of my biggest questions: How specifically can I help console someone in their grief? I expected each member of the Good Grief Group to say they had been consoled in many ways. I expected to leave that meeting with a tidy list of to-do items for people like me who want to help grieving parents. However, I was naively simplistic in my thinking. There is no such to-do list. To my surprise, "Finding Consolation" was a very difficult topic for the Good Grief Group to discuss. Few means of finding effective consolation were identified. Did this mean there was no hope of ever rising out of the terrible pit of grief? How could these five women, who were getting on with good, productive lives, who laugh and love, not be able to say they had found consolation? What I learned is that nuances of language matter greatly in discussions about grief. I learned that there is a significant difference between the definitions of "comfort" and "consolation," and that I had chosen the wrong words. For them, the word "finding" implied an ending. And these women have certainly taught me that there are no end points for their grief or their yearnings for their babies. There will never be a time in their lives that they'll find or do something that finally enables them to say, "That's it. I'm over it." And "consolation" to them denoted pain that was no longer present. Allison, Audra, Heather, Linda, and Tania, a year and a half after the deaths of their babies, still hurt. Not as intensely, not as overtly as they did at first, but pain is not far from the surface for any of them. These women were being totally honest when they said they couldn't discuss this idea in terms of "finding consolation." What helped them rise out of that terrible valley of the shadow of death were the many instances of being comforted along the grief journey. What I think holds promise in all this is that instances of being comforted can come in as many forms as there are personalities: from dragonflies, books, and hugs; to prayer, writing, talking, and seeing that the baby is remembered and mattered. The possibilities for experiencing comfort are endless. In your search for such instances, be patient, open, diligent, creative, prayerful, and gentle with yourself. The instances will come, and they will help.

Something Good Must Come from This Bad

Audra At first, all I could see after Gabriel died was pain and darkness—I saw no goodness in it. Now I am convinced good things have come to me and to others because of Gabriel. I have found light in the darkness. I am now traveling a new road in my life—one that I wouldn't be on if Gabriel had never been a part of me. And it's a good road. I've been given wonderful opportunities to exert positive change in the world, and I owe it all to Gabriel. I have met new people who bless my life. Because of Gabriel, we who have been touched by his precious life will continue to do good, compassionate things. Gabriel's legacy will be one of goodness and love.

Linda I *could* wallow in self-pity for the rest of my life and never acknowledge anyone else's pain besides my own. I *could* make the rest of my life about pain and suffering. This actually would be the easier thing to do. But I don't want it to be that way. What kind of life would that be for me, my family, and especially my surviving daughter?

I owe it to myself and those I love, but especially to both my daughters, to rise above this tragedy and allow something positive to come from it. I imagine Madison would want me to use this pain to help other families and babies, and that is what I try to do with so much of my life now. And as Kaitlyn grows up, I want her to benefit from my example. I know she learns by watching me. I want to teach her what I have come to know about going on with living and loving after tragedy strikes in life. I want Kaitlyn to learn from her parents' faith that God can take even the most tragic situation and bring good from it. By our example, I hope to teach her to give back to her community and to help when she sees others in need. I believe she will see by my actions and my reactions to grief and loss just how much I have loved as a mother, and to teach her she also has this great capacity.

Heather I came to realize rather quickly that if I'm ever to journey through all the bad that is associated with Connor's death, I must make some good come from it. That good won't happen on its own.

I hope to make Connor's life and death the inspiration required to spur our society to pursue the medical research needed to end prematurity once and for all. Then other babies and parents will not have to experience death and loss like we have. For those parents who will still suffer the deaths of their babies, I hope that this book will provide them with solace and guidance. I have learned from and been bettered by Connor, and I know that I can create positive change by sharing his and my story. I hope that through what I have written and shared, people will come to know Connor, remember Connor, and be touched in some positive way by his existence.

Connor's death has already worked some good in my life, and that is the bond of friendship that I have formed with the women of the Good Grief Group. They have all been true blessings in my life. I am so thankful for each one of them and I admire how they each strive to make good happen, and in so doing, honor their beautiful babies.

At the same time, I can look at my daughter Hayden's life as something good that rose from bad. I know that must be a strange thing to say, because Hayden in no way replaces Connor, and in no way do I wish for one child over another. I simply know that if Connor had been born full-term, I physically could not have conceived Hayden when I did. She might not be here today, as we know her now, if Connor had lived. My dream for Connor to live and to be a big brother to Hayden did not come true. But Hayden can be considered, in my mind, as the purest good that came from the terrible loss of her big brother.

Allison The terrible pain of death and grief covers everything in life for a while, but as I come out from underneath those covers, I crave to do good in the world. Good must follow the bad in order for any of it to make sense to me.

Therefore, I deliberately work to take my pain and do something good with it. I am writing this book. I am involved in community service projects. I volunteer for the March of Dimes in an effort to prevent premature birth. I help certain people at work whom I probably never would have reached out to before. I focus on living a more meaningful life. I work to build better friendships. I work to build a more loving family. I live now to be able to say at the end of my life journey, "It is all good."

Tania On many days, I can see no good that comes from this terrible thing that happened to my daughter and family. My lovely daughter, my Lanika, is gone—what could possibly ever be good about this? But after two years of living with this reality, I have learned the only way to live again is to make something good happen because of it. If I don't make something good from my pain and tears, all will be meaningless, empty, and dark. The only way to bring light back to my life is for me to do something good for my family and for other families. I take what Lanika taught me—about who I am, what a family is, what a true friend is, and what true caring is—and try to give more love to this difficult world. It is not hard at all to find people who are hurting, and I want to now be the one to help and comfort them. Because Lanika's heart beats through me, new goodness beats through me.

SOMETHING GOOD MUST COME FROM THIS BAD

REFLECTIONS

FOR THE GRIEVING PARENT:
Have you found yourself with any new passions in life since the death of your baby? If yes, what are your new passions?

FOR THE FAMILY AND FRIENDS OF A GRIEVING PARENT:
What actions have you taken in your own life to make something good come from the tragedy of this child's death? Have you supported your loved ones if they have voiced and/or acted upon new passions?

Vicky Adversity can often spur us into action. The very name these grieving women chose to call our group, the "Good Grief Group," clearly expresses their desire to make something good come of their loss. I believe they all understood early in their grief that if nothing good came from it, all would be for naught. They each deliberately chose not to let this happen. Our Good Grief Group has become just what our name says: *good*. The amazing friendships forged are deep and will be for life. The support they have given one another these past two years has greatly surpassed expectations. The actions they have been spurred into — community volunteering, enlightened parenting, producing something in printed form worth leaving behind — have made this world a better place. Spurred into action by their common adversity, our Good Grief Group has journeyed together toward a more peaceful place. I hope other grieving parents will be inspired by them and follow their example. These grieving mothers have made sure that in the wake of Gabriel, Connor, Madison, Lanika, and Brennen's death, a legacy of good follows.

Bitter or Better?

Tania There is a time in grief, after you lose a baby, when you know you have to make a choice: *Will I be bitter for the rest of my life, or will I choose to make myself and my life better?* The way I see it, I became both. I was bitter at first. When I was broken apart, everything was bitter, even me. I was even bitter at Allah for a while, but as time moved on, and I put the pieces of myself back together, I became better. Much better. Lanika gave me the courage to use my grief to look into myself. I examined my behavior, and my priorities. I found myself in this process. I learned to be more in control of myself, and to treat others with more kindness and compassion than I ever had before. I learned so much about true friendship, and I came to love my friends more deeply because I now know how much they mean to me. They are precious pearls in life. I stopped being bitter at Allah, and my faith is better now. And I looked at what kind of mother I was. I learned how very precious my two other daughters are and how important it is to raise them with all the love I can give them. I came to love and care for them in a whole new way. Lanika surely has made me a better mother. Yes, I am better now than I was before.

Allison Choosing better over bitter is a daily choice. I look around and I see so many people with babies who take having children for granted: celebrities with drug and mental disorders, local teens with no means of supporting a family, or the lady in front me at the grocery store with one infant in the stroller and another on the way in her pregnant belly. But I have a good job, a stable home and marriage, insurance, and so much love to give a child. And yet, my child was taken from me. How can I not be bitter? If I allowed things to progress naturally, I might always be bitter. This would be the easier path to follow. But I don't want that. I don't want my beautiful son's life to change me for the worse. He was all about good things to come. I choose better over bitter to honor my son.

Linda After losing a baby, there is an almost daily choice present in my life—whether I'm going to let this tragedy make me bitter or better. Some days I find I give in to the bitterness. Other days, I find the strength to rise above it and be better. I have found it much harder to choose "better-ness." To make my life better requires action on my part. It takes willpower and energy, and these are hard to find sometimes. In his book *Don't Waste Your Sorrows*, author Paul Billheimer writes about using bad experiences in life to help others. This is what I am trying to do with the loss of Madison. I don't want to waste my sorrow in bitterness.

I volunteer at two different NICUs, helping current parents through the ups and downs of the NICU experience. Each year, I walk in the March of Dimes' March for Babies, to raise money to reduce the incidence of prematurity. Our Good Grief Group gets involved in different projects that help families who either have babies in the NICU or have had babies pass away. We try very hard to use our collective experiences to help as many people in as many different ways as we can: We coordinate the "Path of Hope" every year at the Dallas March for Babies event, we give presentations to hospital NICU staffs on how to care for bereaved families, and we lobby congressmen for laws favorable to babies and families. And in my mothering of Kaitlyn, I know to treasure every moment I have with her, more than I think I would have before. I am not a bitter mom, I am a better mom.

So I choose, even though it's hard, better-ness over bitterness. In the most ironic way, coping with Madison's death has taught me how to live.

Audra Bitter can be a catalyst for better. In grief, bitterness comes first. It's a personal choice to let better follow.

Heather When confronting infant loss, I think you have three choices:

(1) To do nothing and remain completely unchanged by the event
(2) To be bitter and angry
(3) To be better by trying to make something good come from the loss

I can't imagine being completely unchanged, but I think a few do choose that route (*or* maybe their grief just totally paralyzes them into that mode of existence).

I would be lying if I said I didn't have moments of bitterness. I do. I think it's the knee-jerk reaction to grief. I have to fight bitterness, particularly when faced with someone else's pure joy over their pregnancy or birth of their child. I hate that I have these feelings. I never used to be this way. I don't want to harbor bitter feelings, because I am certainly happy for them. But they make me recognize things that I'll never have again: innocence, untethered happiness, no fear. I begin to question, "Why not me? Why wasn't that my life and my story?" I have to work really hard to put my bitter feelings aside. I even gave up being bitter as my pledge for Lent in the first year of my grief. While others were giving up chocolate, beer, or caffeine, I decided to give up bitterness. And every one of those forty days I had to remind myself, when the bitter feelings started creeping in, that I was giving those up. I wasn't going to let them rule my feelings. And I think it was a good exercise. Because I chose to fight it purposefully and intently, I believe that I am better able to push it away when those feelings arise. I do not want to be bitter. It wasn't a part of me in my past, and I don't want it to be a part of me in my future.

Overall, I am choosing "better" as my response to grief. Jerry Sittser writes about a soul finding new graces through grief in his book, *A Grace Disguised*. This thought brings me some peace in this grief journey because I see it happening in me. Grief has deepened my capacity to feel love, joy, happiness, sorrow, empathy, appreciation, and responsibility. I do see that my soul has expanded, and this contributes to me being a better wife, mother, daughter, sister, friend, and person in general. I don't want Connor's life to result in bitterness. I want his memory to push me towards better. This is what I want. This is what I choose.

BITTER OR BETTER?

REFLECTIONS

FOR THE GRIEVING PARENT:
Describe the feelings of bitterness you've had since your baby died. How have you dealt with the bitterness you've felt? Describe instances where you've had to choose between being bitter or being better.

FOR THE FAMILY AND FRIENDS OF A GRIEVING PARENT:
Think about a time in your life where you were bitter about something. What helped you overcome that bitterness? How can what you've learned in your own past about bitterness help you with the bitterness your loved one may be struggling with right now?

Vicky Grief is a very long journey, and as you go along that journey, you leave a trail. What kind of trail do you want to leave behind for your children, for your family and friends? There is opportunity in grief, just as there is opportunity in other adversities. If one chooses to waste their grief in unending bitterness, then the trail they leave behind for others will lead merely to despair. On the other hand, if one chooses to expand their soul and become a wiser, better person, then the trail they leave behind for others to follow will lead to goodness. They will leave an example of love, compassion, faith, and hope. The benefits can be enormous. It may not be the easier trail to forge, and it will take great energy and willpower. But it is the path that directs the griever, and anyone else who follows their trail, toward a healing place.

I Will Always Love, Honor, and Remember My Child

Linda I will always remember Madison. It is no exaggeration to say that I remember her each day. Even though she died, my love for her never will. It is without bounds. I don't believe life is about how long one lives, but rather, what type of impact one has on the people around them. Madison could have lived a long life and not have made the impact she did in the two short days she was with us. My heart will always be broken somewhere because the piece of my heart that is Madison's is in heaven. My hope is that one day my heart will be whole again when I join her in paradise. I will always be thankful that God allowed her to come into my life, even for a brief moment, because that brief time goes on in love into eternity.

Before having my daughters, I never really thought about living my life in a way that would honor someone. Now I do. I want Madison to look down upon me from heaven and be pleased with what I am doing to honor her memory. I strive to honor her in the way I live my life now, and in the way I take care of her sister. Honoring her is a privilege, and I don't feel that I will ever do enough to give her the honor she deserves. But I am going to try!

Allison I am moving forward with my life, and I'm finding ways to "take Brennen along" with me. I need to know my beautiful son is not left behind, unremembered. We have photos of him in our home, we have planted a tree in his memory, I wear dragonfly jewelry that reminds me of him, we form a team in his honor every year for the March of Dimes' March for Babies, and I am writing this book for him. In my remembrance of Brennen, I have come to a peaceful realization: What makes Brennen unique and special is that he is sacred. Part of the definition of sacred is "to be set apart." As his mother, it is hard to accept that Brennen is set apart from us, but I have a peaceful awareness knowing he is now sacred. This is a beautiful way for me to remember my son.

As important as it is for me to do things in memory of Brennen, I cannot express in words what it means when the significant people in my life also love, honor, and remember Brennen. I truly enjoy hearing about these things, whether it's a friend's daughter wearing a "Brennen badge" that I made for the March of Dimes around town, loved ones celebrating a memorial service, or my mother organizing a March of Dimes' March for Babies in her hometown. I draw peace and love from hearing when things like this happen. So to all my friends and family, keep remembering and loving Brennen in your lives. Keep showing and telling me when you do!

Heather On the day of Connor's funeral, I felt like I was in a fog, and I don't remember much, but I do remember that so many people attended the ceremony that the chapel overflowed with guests. The generous outpouring of love and prayer for Connor and our family was overwhelming. It was a beautiful way for them to honor Connor. But as time passed, most of those who supported us that day slipped back into their normal lives. To us, it seemed as if they forgot about Connor and our experience. It took us a long while to see that it wasn't up to them to continually remember Connor. It was ours to do. We were his parents. We will always love Connor—it's automatic, like breathing.

But how to make sure he is not forgotten and honored was more of a challenge. I am very grateful to the few who didn't seemingly forget so quickly and easily. I know I don't give near enough credit to those who continued to grieve with me and for me, who listened to me, and helped me in remembering and honoring Connor. I am extremely grateful for the shoulders I was given to cry on, for the remembrance gifts given to me (poems, cards, verses), songs shared, the candles lit, the photos hung in homes, for unsolicited tributes of his life, donations given in his memory, and the acknowledgements on anniversaries. Many people continued to remember and honor Connor along with Cole and me. All this brings me so much peace, and I am ever thankful for it.

It is very important for me personally to do things that honor and remember my son. The March of Dimes has given me the most opportunity to publicly acknowledge, remember, and honor Connor's life. I am thankful for them and grateful to them for what they do.

To incorporate Connor's memory in our home, we display photos and keepsakes around the house, we built a memory garden in honor of Connor in our backyard, and we light a candle and say a special prayer for him at Thanksgiving. Our Good Grief Group planted a tree in a park by a playground to remember our angel babies. As a group, we have reached out to several other mothers who have lost babies and tried to be of comfort to them.

Is this enough? No. I am afraid whatever I do will never be enough. Isn't this a universal feeling that most mothers have about their children—we never quite do enough for them? I am certain that I'm meant to do more, and I will look for ways to do this throughout my life. I acknowledge and accept Connor's death. I have to. But I also acknowledge his life, and will always try to honor it. It touches me deeply when my friends and family do the same.

Audra It is very important to me to do many things to remember and honor my son. I am always grateful when others around me join in remembering, because it alleviates some of my worry that I might somehow forget him someday. After I finish doing something for Gabe's memory and honor, I feel like I've just taken a cleansing breath. I need to know I'm doing something for him, and when I'm done, I feel purged, soothed by action, and lifted by love.

Tania I have three daughters, two with me here, and one in heaven. I will always love all three of them. When I buy something for my two daughters here, I buy Lanika a flower. Lanika is in a garden now, how can she be without flowers? I honor Lanika through contributing to the March of Dimes so that other babies will be spared premature beginnings. I give to needy people, donate to my mosque, and feed orphans. This way, Lanika's life is honored and remembered. I think about Lanika with my every breath, for she is a part of me. When people speak Lanika's name, it makes me very happy, because I know she still exists in their mind. She is not here, but she goes on, my love for her goes on…forever.

I WILL ALWAYS LOVE, HONOR, AND REMEMBER MY CHILD

REFLECTIONS

FOR THE GRIEVING PARENT:
What ways have you found to honor and remember your baby? Which ways mean the most to you, and why? Who among your friends and family do you find the most comfort in doing these things with? Why?

FOR THE FAMILY AND FRIENDS OF A GRIEVING PARENT:
Your loved one doesn't want to be alone in remembering and honoring their baby. In what ways do you join them in honoring and remembering their child?

Vicky Because the circle of witnesses to their lives was small, the world might not have noticed, nor long remembered Gabriel, Connor, Madison, Lanika, and Brennen. I believe that would have been a terrible shame. Don't we all desire witnesses to our lives, someone to take notice of who we are and what we do? Don't we all wish to be remembered in some way, to have some significance? These babies did not have a chance to leave a song, a book, or a painting behind for posterity. Their parents were their greatest witnesses, and their parents profoundly experienced their significance. No wonder the parental desires to always love, honor, and remember their babies are so fundamental to Audra, Heather, Linda, Tania, and Allison's being now.

Whether this remembrance is a lit candle, a back yard garden, or a campaign to improve the lives of others, these grieving parents continually give witness to their children. In so doing, these loving mothers rekindle their own inner spirits. They are better for it; the world is better for it. By reading this book, you have now been made witness to Gabriel, Connor, Madison, Lanika, and Brennen's lives. Through them your mind has been enlightened about surviving loss, journeying through grief, and helping a grieving loved one. Take this new knowledge and make your life, or someone else's life, the better for it.

Peace and the Sundial

*M*ore than two years have passed now since Gabriel, Connor, Madison, Lanika, and Brennen came into my life. I cared for these precious babies and families as a nurse when they lived; I cared for their beautiful mothers as a friend after they died. The six of us women have met on a journey. Shoulder to shoulder and hand in hand, we pointed our hearts in the direction of peace. Each one of our lives has changed along the way—because of grief, but also because of life itself. Grief does not happen in a vacuum. It does not happen in a static, unchanging world. Amongst the Good Grief Group these past several years, careers have changed, babies have been born, marriages have been altered, surviving children have matured, other loved ones have died, and life has gone on, bringing (like it always does) both joy and sorrow. In their search for healing, I have seen a wisdom grow in Audra, Heather, Linda, Tania, and Allison. The truth of an inscription on a sundial I once read has not escaped them:

"Peace is not the absence of conflict from life,
but the ability to cope with it."

They know the peace they seek is not some magical pot of gold to be found at the end of a rainbow. No one can give peace to them. They realize surviving loss is not about finding a silver lining to a dark cloud, but about reaching for calm amid the chaos. They've learned the journey toward peace is a lifelong undertaking, and that it's imperative to continue loving deeply, living well, and finding greater purpose for their lives along the way. They are aware that difficulties will never be totally absent from their lives, and that much of whether or not they find joy again depends on their ability to cope with the difficulties. The Good Grief Group has been brave, creative, patient, spiritual, and persistent in finding ways to cope with the loss of their babies and their immense grief. As we came to the end of our structured writing gatherings, I thought it best to end in a similar way as we started—with a list. Two years ago, I asked the mothers to tell me what they thought were the hardest things about grieving the loss of their babies. That list filled eight pages of a large, spiral notebook. For over two years now, we've examined and written about the items on that list. So I asked Audra, Heather, Linda, Tania, and Allison to collectively list actions they believed to be helpful in their grief walk towards peace. Like their first list two years ago, this new list was extensive. The Good Grief Group found many concrete, constructive actions that grieving parents can use to seek healing after an infant's death. Maybe some of their ways can become your ways. This is their list.

FIND CALM AMID THE CHAOS
- Listen to inspiring or soothing songs.
- Envision your baby in heaven.
- Sit in your back yard and listen to the birds.
- Find regular quiet time to journal your thoughts about your baby and your grief.
- Take a long nap when you feel worn down.
- Take a walk with a special friend on a pretty day.
- Wear a special piece of jewelry that reminds you of your baby.
- Take a long, hot bath at the end of a particularly hard day.
- Cuddle with your dog or cat when you feel down.
- Find comfort in dragonflies, or some other creation in nature that reminds you of your child.
- Talk to your spouse, minister, significant loved ones, or a professional grief counselor about your baby and your grief. Don't go it alone. Talk, talk, talk!

READ BOOKS THAT CAN HELP YOU IN YOUR GRIEF
We found comfort in:
- *The Hiding Place* by Corrie Ten Boom
- *A Grace Disguised* by Jerry Sittser
- *Traveling Light* by Max Lucado
- *Don't Waste Your Sorrows* by Paul Billheimer
- *Man's Search for Meaning* by Viktor Frankl
- Any biography of people who have survived difficult times

LIVE WELL
- Find new hobbies with which you can enjoy life more.
- Sing out heartily when you hear a good song on the radio or at church.
- Be inspired by great art. Meditate on *The Pieta* by Michelangelo.
- Hug your spouse often, but especially when you're feeling down.
- Be inspired by great quotes.
- Make new friends.
- Eat healthy.
- Cry when you need to. Find safe places to cry like the shower or your car.
- Set new life goals with your spouse.
- Start a new habit: Tell significant people in your life often how much you love them.
- Go back to the NICU and tell the doctors and nurses who cared for your baby how much you appreciate them.
- Find ways to release your anger in healthy ways: throw rocks into a pond, punch a punching bag, work out at the gym, or go for a jog.

FIND GREATER PURPOSE FOR YOUR LIFE

- Help another grieving person through their grief.
- Become less materialistic.
- Spend more time working to help people in your community and less time watching TV.
- Redefine your priorities in life.
- Lobby legislators for causes that are important to you.
- Be on a parent panel to teach nurses and doctors how to care for bereaved families.
- Raise funds for research that fights prematurity and birth defects.
- Write a book that can help someone.
- Start a new outreach ministry at your church.
- Volunteer for the March of Dimes.
- Donate to an orphanage.

STRENGTHEN YOUR FAITH

- Go to church, get to know your minister better, and find inspiration in sermons.
- Have friends from your mosque pray for your baby.
- Read Psalm 23.
- Give up bitterness for Lent.
- Read the Bible or Qur'an.
- Fast.
- Become part of a neighborhood Bible study group.
- Write a prayer to say for your baby during the holidays.
- Find Scripture verses that inspire you and answer questions you have about death, grief, and suffering.

MEMORIALIZE YOUR BABY IN BEAUTIFUL WAYS

- Build a backyard garden in your baby's memory.
- Hang photographs of your baby in your house and carry one with you in your wallet.
- Have a remembering tradition on your baby's birthday (release balloons or make a special meal every year on that day).

- Have a remembering tradition on your baby's anniversary of death (take gifts to the NICU or release butterflies—they can be purchased online).
- Write a poem for your baby.
- Walk in the March of Dimes' March for Babies every year in memory of your baby.
- Make your baby's memory a part of your family holiday traditions (buy a new ornament for your baby every year for your Christmas tree, or have a special candle symbolizing your baby on your dining room table at Thanksgiving).

Two Specific Ways the Good Grief Group Memorialized Their Babies Together as a Group

Candles and Stones: The Good Grief Group started every meeting with each mother lighting a white candle in memory of their child. The candles were interspersed in the middle of the table among stones on which their baby's names were engraved. The lit candles always reminded us that this endeavor was undertaken out of love for these cherished babies. Throughout our meetings, the mothers would often gently rub the stone with their baby's name on it—it is so important to see your baby's name on something permanent and tangible.

Tree Planting: The Good Grief Group arranged, through our local parks and recreation department, to have a tree planted in a park near a pond and baseball diamond in memory of their angel babies. A bronze plaque is placed by the tree with the baby's names engraved on it. It has been a soothing thing for all the Good Grief Group families to watch that tree grow strong and to see it shade the path along which many children stroll and play.

PEACE AND THE SUNDIAL

REFLECTIONS

FOR THE GRIEVING PARENT:
List the ways you are coping as you travel your grief journey.

FOR THE FAMILY AND FRIENDS OF A GRIEVING PARENT:
In what ways have you helped your loved one find personally effective ways to cope with their grief?

Vicky I began this book with the admission that I really knew very little about how a parent grieved in the aftermath of infant death. But I had a burning desire to understand. I asked Audra, Heather, Linda, Tania, and Allison to teach me everything they could about their grief. I deeply desired to broaden my understanding of their grief so that I might more effectively help them and others. These truly remarkable women bared their hearts to me at vulnerable, low points in their lives. I am deeply honored that they trusted me at a time when it was difficult for them to place their trust in anything or anyone. I have come to learn that journeying through this type of grief requires tremendous courage and energy. Before I came to know these mothers, I had no inkling as to the overwhelming depth of their profound grief.

These mothers taught me much as I opened my heart to their pain, and as I remained available to them in their grief. What have I come to know because of what we've shared these past several years? I now believe that grieving the death of a baby is quite possibly the most difficult life experience one might face in life. I also believe one can survive it. One can find joy again. How is this possible? Why do I think this? I believe wholeheartedly that there is a good and gracious God loving us through the joys and sorrows of our lives. God's presence is always there, if we just look and listen. I believe in the resiliency of the human spirit and that it can be rekindled when something tragic in life causes its inner flame to go out. I believe in the bonds of family and the powers of friendship which can carry a person through their darkest hours. I believe our children are one of the greatest blessings we are gifted with in this world, and that they enrich our lives tremendously. I believe we are all meant throughout our existence to love in such a way that transforms lives. I believe brief instances in life can have lifelong impacts. I believe tears are a good and necessary thing. I believe being present by listening to grieving people is almost always better than trying to say wise things, giving advice, or trying to fix it. I believe that life may end, but love never does. I believe that we are not meant just for this world—that there is something far better awaiting us when our earthly lives are over, and this is why we can hope. I believe all our tears will be wiped away in heaven by the tender hand of God. I believe love bears all things, hopes all things, and endures all things. I believe we're all in this life together, and we are meant to be holding one another up throughout the difficulties we face. No one should be alone in their sorrows. If we all love one another unconditionally, without reluctance or under compulsion, God will provide us with every blessing we need. I know this all to be true. Gabriel and Audra; Connor and Heather; Madison and Linda; Lanika and Tania; and Brennen and Allison have a message to deliver to us all. They are truly angels who gathered in my midst, and they profoundly enlightened me.

It is my fervent prayer and hope that these angels have enlightened you as well.

Parting Words

From the Mothers

My dearest Gabriel,
My sweet angel boy,

The moment I found out you were coming, you changed me. The first time I felt you move, you changed me. The moment I saw your precious little face, you changed me. And when I kissed you goodbye…I was forever changed. The way I think, feel, and act today is all because of the love and blessings you have brought into my life. I'm forever grateful that you are my son. I would endure this terrible pain a thousand times over just to have our time together. I think of you daily and carry you in my heart always. You are my most precious gift and most abundant blessing. I love you with all that I am, and in my heart I know that my love finds you, comforts and cradles you like I wish my arms could. I dream about how life would be and what it would be like to know you. You'd be three soon and oh the happy trouble you would be. I strive daily to be someone you would be proud of, someone deserving of being a mother to such a perfect being. I do my best to honor your memory and make sure that, while your time on earth may be done, that your story continues. There are so many things to say but no words to do them justice. Oh, how I wish I could hold you just once more.

Mommy loves you angel,

Mommy

Dear Connor,

You were so wanted and loved and I will love you my entire lifetime. I have accepted that you don't live here with me on this earth, but I will always grieve your absence from me. I miss you. I mourn that I did not get the chance to know you, but I look forward to meeting you in heaven where you now live on in perfect peace. Your life and death changed me forever, and I will always strive to make that change be for the better. I am sorry you suffered so much during the twenty days you lived on earth—if I could have taken that pain away from you, I most surely would have. I know that your last day of life was a glorious day for you, and for that I am grateful. I will never forget loving you into heaven—you passed so comfortably from my arms into peace. Because of you, Connor, I feel more, love more, question more, cry more—all of which are good things. Your father and I will take these gifts you left us and lead more purposeful lives. We will teach your sister Hayden to live a good and purposeful life as well. I know you were meant to come and go in my life the painfully brief way you did, but I still ask why and try to understand. In this life, I will never totally understand—whatever the answers are wouldn't be enough for me here anyway. Your life was a precious gift to me, Connor, and I will always work toward sharing your goodness in the world around me. Thank you, Connor, for the gift you have been to me.

With all my love,

Mom

Dear Madison,

It has been two and a half years since I have seen your precious little face. The memory of your face is seared in my mind, and I can see you any time I close my eyes. I wish it were that easy to be with you. Madison, I think about you every single day. There is never a moment I don't long for you to be in my arms. I try to imagine what it will be like in heaven, when I will finally get to see and hold you. That will be my perfect peace. As your sister Kaitlyn grows, I wonder if your eyes would have been the electric blue that hers are, or what trouble the two of you would have made as a team ganging up on me. What I do know is that you gave your sister so much strength, and I thank you for that. Our entire family hurts because you are not here, but none of us would take back one second we shared with you, to spare ourselves the sorrow we now bear because of your absence. The pain we feel is evidence of the tremendous love we have for you. You have changed us as a family, and we will always do things to honor your memory. We love you, Maddy, and you will never be out of our hearts.

Love,

Momma

Dear Lanika,

I don't know how to start this letter to you, even though I have spoken to you so very many times in my thoughts. I have talked to you in my sad times, in my happy times, in my sleep, in my dreams, in the daylight, and in the darkness. And every time I have talked to you, it felt to me as if you were smiling down on me. It has been more than two years that you are gone, and the emptiness still remains and hurts. I want you to know that you are always with me, with our family, every millisecond. Your sisters often talk about you, wondering what you would have looked like in a pretty dress we see, or how fun it would have been to push you in a stroller, or what it would have been like to have you with us during our happy family times. You continue to have a place in our family. You are attached to us always. I often wonder what your being must be like now…. Heaven must be really beautiful, and I love to think of you dancing happily around there. You looked so pretty with your white Hezab on—that is a peaceful memory I have of you. Lanika, you taught and brought me so many things, and I am so thankful for you. You made me strong—stronger than I ever thought I could be. Because of you, I have been blessed with friends who truly care. They give me strength and love in my life. When I need a shoulder to cry on, they are always there for me. They have helped me breathe again after you left, when I didn't think it was possible to do so. I know there will be a day when I will be with you again, and I am waiting for that day. Until then, I know you see me from heaven. Sometimes at night I look at the stars in the sky. When a star twinkles, I feel it's you smiling at us. Lanika, my lovely daughter, I miss you so much.

With my every breath, I love you,

Your Ammani

Dear Brennen,

I want to tell you how different my existence is now that you came into my life. You motivated, challenged, changed, and inspired me to a higher level of being in all that I am: mother, wife, daughter, sister, teacher, and friend. The incredible love experience I shared with you has not only taught me much about myself, but I have also learned so much about your Daddy and all those with whom we share our lives. I love you so much Brennen. This love story between you and me began long before I met you. Even though I did not yet know what you looked like, and I hadn't looked into your beautiful eyes or held your tiny hand, I felt a deep love for you, my child within my womb. Long before I even knew your name, I was determined always to protect you and keep you safe. My overwhelming love for you only intensified after I laid eyes on your precious nose, stroked your curly hair, and held your tiny hand in mine. Every time I spoke your name, my love for you grew stronger and deeper. I treasure the few precious days we spent together, but I am sad that they are all I have to hold on to. I wanted so much more time with you, to see your smile, and to hear your laugh. But the deep love connection we share and the blessings that fill my life because of you live on strong as ever. My dear, dear son, you are within my heart always.

With all my love,

Mom

From Vicky

Dear Gabriel, Connor, Madison, Lanika, and Brennen,

Your lives were the beginning of a beautiful song. Your mothers have now written the lyrics. You precious angels, who gathered in my midst, have left behind a message that sings out loudly from the pages of this book.

- For grieving parents: Please know you are not alone in your grief journey, and you will find your way to survive your pain. Be courageous, patient, and faithful, for God cares for you and will not leave you abandoned in your sorrows.

- For family and friends of a grieving parent: Care for your grieving loved one tenderly, quietly, and without judgment. No one should have to grieve alone—you are very much needed right now. Do not ignore or try to minimize your loved one's pain, but lovingly walk beside them as they carry it throughout their lives.

Dear sweet angel babies, your lives, your mothers, your families, and your message have enlightened me. I will do my best to keep on singing your beautiful song to whoever may be helped by hearing it.

With great love,

Vicky

The Gathering

June 2006

Victoria (Vicky) Leland, RN

In June of 2006, I celebrated my nineteenth year in NICU bedside nursing. By that time in my career, I had branched out from my bedside clinical work as a nurse and become a published author and photographer, hoping these creative pursuits would help me be more effective in assisting NICU families. During my career, I saw high drama unfold within the quiet rooms of my NICU, making me part of so many families' great triumphs and joys, as well as their tragic sufferings and sorrow. To be honest, it was a vocation I entered with a reluctant heart because (and I know this must sound strange from a nurse) I don't like hospitals. But what I found as I grew in my vocation was that *I love the people in hospitals*. Out of that love grew a passion to be as much of an instrument of healing and comfort to these NICU babies and families as I could. It is my sincere belief that God puts me where God wants me, and it is no mere coincidence when my path crosses a certain baby and family's path in life. I have been tremendously blessed over two decades of nursing, coming to love and be loved by so many truly wonderful NICU babies and families. Many still send me Christmas cards, some call and visit me occasionally, a few have become lifelong friends. I have become a godmother to two of my former patients, and I have had a baby named after me. In spending so many years "protesting the darkness" (as I have come to call it) of all the suffering prematurity and birth defects cause, I was blessed to feel the glow of great satisfaction and joy from my nursing care, photography, and writing efforts.

But as I celebrated my nineteenth year in this vocation, little did I know how frequently I would be "tested in the darkness" by being witness to so many infant deaths in the coming months. Our unit had a dramatic increase in the number of severely premature births that year, resulting in a higher number of infant deaths. As I repeatedly saw so much death and grief, my faith in a merciful God was tested but ultimately strengthened. My own search for the meaning

185

of life and the purpose of suffering was intensified, but I eventually found clarification. The pain and suffering I repeatedly witnessed left me acutely aware of the need to find better, more effective ways of dealing with heartache and loss. I was changed profoundly by the experiences of that year, and was compelled to step beyond the scope of my usual care and interaction with my patients.

I can almost pinpoint the moment when this change first started to take place in me. It was that Christmas, as I sat in the stillness of midnight Mass listening to a beautiful rendition of "Silent Night." Unexpectedly, the words of this timeless Christmas lullaby overtook me, as if I was hearing them for the very first time:

> *Silent night, holy night*
> *Mother and child*
> *Sleep in heavenly peace.*

These words triggered flashbacks to the tragic events of the past year—of the grieving families I'd tended to that year, the mothers clutching their dying children, the baby funerals where they had talked about babies now sleeping in heavenly peace. The pain I had restrained as I tried to be strong for others freely flowed down my cheeks that Christmas night. This was not typical of me. I left Mass resolved to do more. I fervently prayed to God that night for fewer infant deaths in the coming year, but if more dying babies were to cross my path, I asked to be given the grace needed to be an instrument of comfort and healing to them and their families. The gathering of angels that crossed my path in 2006 and into 2007 assisted me in finding that grace. Together we helped one another find a way out of the darkness and toward the comfort and healing that we all so desperately needed.

And the first angel, appropriately enough, was named Gabriel.

Gabriel and his mother Audra

Gabriel was born fifteen weeks premature to a young couple just starting out in life together. Gabriel's father Erik (recently returned from a military tour of duty in Iraq) and mother Audra (a bank employee) were extremely excited to start a family. Although Gabriel arrived premature, he faired remarkably well, needing surprisingly little of the medical assistance most babies his age and size require. His doctor even nicknamed him "Superman." I took photographs of him and his parents in those early days, rejoicing with them in their good fortune. There was even talk at one point about his going home, maybe in three or four weeks, if all continued well.

But then tragedy struck. A particularly devastating and little understood complication of prematurity called necrotizing enterocolitis caused most of Gabriel's intestines to suddenly die. Even though he was whisked off to emergency surgery, most of his intestines had to be removed. For three weeks after the surgery, Gabriel fought gallantly to overcome this insult to his little body, his distraught parents at his bedside. Gabriel died while being held lovingly in his mother's arms at sixty-two days of age.

I was Gabriel's nurse some days during those last weeks of his life. At times, I peered into his little eyes, seeing a lovely spirit and soul staring back at me. A father of another baby adjacent to Gabriel's bed remarked to me one day, "I've watched you caring for Gabriel. You really do love him, don't you?" He was correct in his observation: I did. My heart broke as Gabriel slowly slipped away from us. I ached for Audra and Erik as I attended doctor conferences with them where they had to make nightmarish decisions about Gabriel's care. This young couple was the age of my own daughter, and I felt a very maternal concern for them as they endured this suffering. On the day Gabriel died, I sat with them a bit as they held their dying son. I looked into their eyes and knew something died within them too.

After Gabriel's death, I periodically saw Audra at hospital memorial services and March of Dimes events. I read some of what she blogged about her beloved son. I found her eloquent in expressing her love for Gabriel and wise beyond her years about death and mourning. She had suffered the loss of other loved ones in her life before, most significantly her father when she was eight. I saw in Audra remarkable strength and resiliency, responding bravely to a world that has often been very harsh to her. I saw that Audra's generous heart and stubborn strength would never allow her to be beaten down by the difficult world. She, like her son, is an angel.

August 2006

Connor and his mother Heather

Connor was born twenty-four weeks into his mother's pregnancy (a full-term pregnancy lasts forty weeks) to a couple who had spent their first ten years out of college building a happy, well-planned life. Cole was part-owner in a newly formed company, and Heather was an engineer at a major telecommunications corporation. Married for seven years, it seemed everything they ever wanted, planned, and worked for in life came to them. They never imagined that their first-born would arrive severely premature. Despite all their best efforts, and for no reason ever determined, Connor arrived at twenty-four weeks gestation—barely beyond the point in a pregnancy when babies can sometimes be saved. Connor struggled from the onset of his brief life, his lungs and immune system simply too immature to sustain him. Medical technology was ineffective at helping him.

My path first crossed this family's life when Connor was about a week and a half old as his struggle for survival intensified and as his major organs began to fail. By that time, he was on drugs that kept his muscles from moving. I never had the chance to peer into Connor's eyes as I had with Gabriel. At times when I was alone with him, I studied his delicate little hands and admired his beautiful face. I took photographs of Connor's hands in his parents' hands, and felt his essence was captured there. Although fate prevented me from ever knowing his personality, I was able to admire his angelic face and came to love his dear soul all the same.

I distinctly remember my first encounter with Heather. We shared an introductory handshake across Connor's bed and a knowing locking of eyes. As I shook her hand, the fear and anxiety pulsed from her, and I knew that her heart was breaking. I think that as we touched physically, she could feel my concern, that I cared, and that I intended to help her through whatever lay ahead.

Heather and Cole were only given twenty days with Connor. I was with them a great deal in Connor's final week of life—at his bedside baptism, at conferences with the doctors about his deteriorating condition, and as they were faced with making heart-wrenching decisions about Connor's care. And then, in the long silent hours of a Friday night in August, I sat with Cole and Heather as Connor died in their arms. They both wanted me there at that very difficult time, and I wanted to be there with them. All our hearts broke together that night as Connor slipped very peacefully away. They asked me to photograph them loving Connor into heaven, to give them some tangible memory of the first time—the only time, the last time—they ever held their son. The photographs I took of them that night ended up being incredible portraits of love, and I believe they are the closest thing to something sacred that I have ever photographed. I felt it while I was there with them, and later, viewing the photographs I took of them that night, confirmed it: We shared a holy night.

Heather and I stayed closely in touch after Connor's death, sharing many long lunches, phone conversations, walks, and Starbucks coffees as we rehashed Connor's life and death, trying to make sense of it together. There was a rare immediacy of ease between the two of us, and a lovely friendship grew quickly.

While still in the throes of raw grief, Heather became pregnant again. Although this was a happy event, it tended to magnify her feelings of loss over Connor, as each milestone she reached in the new pregnancy triggered her overwhelming memories and love for Connor. After a very anxious nine-month second pregnancy, Heather happily delivered a full-term, healthy baby girl named Hayden. However, the joy over this pregnancy and second child seemed to often be overshadowed by her intense yearning and mourning for

Connor. While I watched Heather bravely be mother to both her children—mourning Connor while joyously welcoming Hayden—I grew to respect her immensely. Her heart knew great suffering, and yet she was fiercely determined to make some good come of this tragedy. She gave speeches with me to NICU staffs on how to help families whose babies were dying. Together she and I lobbied Texas legislators for laws favorable to premature babies. She joined the efforts of the March of Dimes to ensure babies are born healthy—all as ways to honor her son. She felt strongly compelled to save other families from the anguish her family suffered. It was as if she shook her hand at death and grief and said to them defiantly, "You will not get the better of me!" She, like her son, is an angel.

August 2006

Madison and her mother Linda

Madison and her twin sister Kaitlyn were born twenty-four weeks into their mother's pregnancy. Madison, who occupied the NICU hospital bed right next to Connor's, died at a mere two days of age before I ever had a chance to meet her. The first time I learned about Madison and met her mother Linda was when I was standing at Connor's bedside with Heather. Linda walked by us as she went to visit Kaitlyn, stopping to tell Heather, "We buried Madison today." I watched these two women, strangers only a few days earlier, now sharing the unbearable with one another. They demonstrated a mutual kindness and understanding. They were lifeboats to one another as they felt themselves sinking in this overwhelming storm of life. I watched them begin a unique and timely friendship born from the untimely deaths of their babies.

Linda and her husband of nine years, Brendan, had eagerly anticipated the arrival of their twin girls. Their premature delivery was completely unexpected, throwing them into a scary, confusing world so unlike anything they had ever known. Neither of them had any medical background, Brendan being a general manager of a boat dealership and Linda being an accountant. Over the course of a few days, they went from carefree bliss, anticipating twins, to the shocking delivery of two babies barely weighing one pound each, to the death and burial of one daughter, to the complicated, up and down NICU rollercoaster journey of their surviving daughter.

Kaitlyn defied the odds and, after a harried four-month stay in my NICU, went home thriving. Her miraculous triumph over her premature beginnings was an incredible joy to Linda and Brendan, and they knew how very blessed they were with Kaitlyn's life and good health. This, however, in no way minimized the intense grief they felt in losing their beloved Madison. They wanted to scream at every well-intentioned person who told them in the throes of their grief, "Well at least you have Kaitlyn." Linda and Brendan knew they were given two daughters—one they now gratefully share their lives with, and one forever gone from their embrace. Every milestone Kaitlyn reached was punctuated with a bittersweet emotion: They relished Kaitlyn's achievements while mourning Madison's absence from ever sharing in their joy.

While I only cared for Kaitlyn a few times in her four-month NICU stay, my shifts while caring for her were on particularly difficult days in her journey. Throughout her stay, I would often stop to check on Kaitlyn and chat with her parents as they experienced the ups and downs that a twenty-four week gestation preemie causes. Linda and Brendan always attended the Parent Support Group meetings that I facilitated. While they themselves struggled through grief, crisis, uncertainty, and worry, I saw them often reach out to other NICU families struggling through difficult times. I was impressed by their compassionate, generous hearts. They rose above their own needs to help others.

Immediately after Kaitlyn's discharge, Linda became very involved as a volunteer, assisting me with my Parent Support Group program. Whereas most parents leave the NICU with relief to go home and start anew, far, far away from the sounds and smells and sufferings seen in the NICU world, Linda didn't miss a beat before she came back to give back. She and her husband had a burning desire to assist other NICU families struggling through what they personally knew to be one of life's most difficult experiences. Linda knew both sides: life and death, joy and sorrow. She was eager to offer a wisdom that few can give, as effective solace to those in need of comfort. She, like her daughter, is an angel.

December 2006

Lanika and her mother Tania

Lanika was the third child (third daughter) born to Tania and Sunny. She arrived thirteen weeks premature, and like Gabriel, did very well her first weeks in the NICU. During those first weeks, when I cared for Lanika, the mood was light. Tania, a social and immediately likable young mother, and I shared many wonderful bedside conversations about our families, raising daughters, and our faiths. Tania and Sunny were from Bangladesh, family oriented, loving parents, and were devout Muslims. Tania would often sit gracefully at Lanika's bedside dressed in her beautiful saris, wearing her prayer shawl and praying from the Qur'an. I was curious to know about her faith, and she was eager to share with me and learn about mine as well. (I am Catholic.) Tania and I enjoyed our talks about faith, both respecting one another's customs and beliefs. In the end, it was apparent to us that Tania and I both pray to the same God (the God of Abraham), just in different ways and traditions. Little did we know, as we leisurely discussed our faiths together in those quiet, promising weeks of Lanika's young life, that both our faiths would be put to the test.

At six weeks of age, Lanika came down with a terribly overwhelming infection. Despite the best that the top infectious disease specialists and high-powered antibiotics could offer, Lanika's immature immune system never overcame this battle. Over the course of three tortuous weeks, the infection raged, and Lanika slipped slowly away from us. Tania and Sunny, who had known such hope for their third daughter, were brokenhearted. They began an almost constant vigil at Lanika's bedside. As I cared for Lanika two days before she died, it was mostly silence shared between Tania and me. There are no adequate words to speak between caring individuals when a child is dying in front of them. Our eyes often met though, and they spoke what our mouths could not. I asked Tania at one point, "I have done everything I can possibly do for Lanika. What can I do for you?" She replied, "Pray, Vicky, please pray for my daughter." Standing on opposite sides of Lanika's bed, Tania and I grasped hands and bowed our heads together over Lanika. I implored Almighty God, in the name of Jesus Christ, and she implored Allah, the Compassionate, the Merciful, and together we asked for healing and good health for Lanika. I felt it to be a powerfully sacred moment shared between this devoutly Muslim mother and this devoutly Catholic nurse.

The specific miracles and healing we prayed for did not come. As I cared for Lanika on the day before she died, I found Tania at the beginning of my shift sitting exhausted at Lanika's bedside, staring unblinkingly into nowhere, unresponsive to words and almost catatonic. After I finished my nursing tasks of caring for Lanika, I turned and tried to care for Tania. When I offered to get her something to eat or drink, Tania spoke the only words she uttered that day: "Vicky, in my faith when we pray most fervently, we fast. I am fasting." I responded, "We Catholics practice that tradition too. I will join you in your fast." For my twelve-hour shift, I joined Tania in eating and drinking nothing. We shared together a day-long fast, which is a beautiful form of prayer. It revealed all Tania and I needed to express to one another. In all my years of living my Catholic faith, this was the very first time I had ever fasted outside the obligatory Good Friday routine fast. A devout Muslim mother taught me the incredible beauty of this form of fervent prayer.

Lanika passed away the next day, with both her parents at her side. The miracles we prayed for—life and good health in this world for Lanika—did not come. However, other miracles of healing for this beautiful family did come. How does healing come to the shattered hearts of parents so ready to give a lifetime of love to their child, only to have that child gone forever from their grasp? I believe this sort of healing is impossible without great love and timely miracles being showered upon their hurting souls.

Tania's grief was every bit of the "dark night of the soul." With remarkable grace though, she faced it bravely by fiercely loving her two surviving daughters, by generously reaching out to assist others in great need and sorrow, and by deepening her faith in the God with whom she knows Lanika peacefully rests now. I came to admire Tania's motherly warmth and generosity of spirit. She, like her daughter, is an angel.

March 2007

Brennen and his mother Allison

Allison endured eight weeks of strict bed rest before delivering her first child, Brennen, at twenty-eight weeks. In the days following Brennen's birth, Allison and her husband, Brian, desperately tried to give their son every chance of survival. They hoped against hope, and they prayed for their miracle, but they still could not save Brennen, who died at nine days of age.

My path first intersected with Brennen's family's when he was six days old and very sick. I remember Allison's mother standing stalwartly by her daughter's side in loving support, even though her own heart was breaking twice over—once for her anguished daughter, and once for her critically-ill grandchild. She looked earnestly into my eyes and said: "You will never meet a finer young couple than Allison and Brian. They have so much love to give this child." It did not take long for me to see that this new grandmother was right. I observed Allison talk to, touch, and be with her son, and I witnessed a remarkable testimony to the love between mother and child. Some mothers are blessed to spend their entire adult lives loving their children but never fill it with the amount of love that Allison shared in nine days with Brennen. She infused his few days with a lifetime of love. At one point in the two shifts in which I cared for Brennen, I was able to take some photographs of this remarkable interaction between Allison and Brennen. It's been said that you cannot claim to really see something until you have photographed it. What I saw as I photographed them together was that the mother did not only love the child in this instance, but the child truly loved the mother as well. Despite all the tubes and wires and buzzing machines surrounding him, Brennen knew he was deeply loved, and he loved equally in return.

Brennen's death came quickly, not allowing time for Allison and Brian to get to his bedside at the precise moment he left us. This heaped tragedy on top of tragedy for this family, because, as hard as it is for parents to hold a dying child, it is harder for parents to be denied that sacred moment. Sadly, this fine couple, with so much love to give this beautiful boy, was doubly robbed by prematurity: robbed of their child and robbed by prematurity's indiscriminant unpredictability.

After I attended Brennen's funeral, I stayed in touch with Allison, occasionally sharing long email messages and lunches with her. I invited her to join me in some volunteer work that I thought would help her find ways to express the truly remarkable love she held for her beloved son. A special education teacher by profession, Allison had a tremendously generous heart. She began almost immediately volunteering to help other NICU families in need, all while still in the throes of deep grief herself. Allison did not live merely for herself, but rather she shared her love generously in life by touching, helping, and healing the many hurting souls who crossed her path. She, like her son, is an angel.

Hidden Presence

I met these five families during their worst nightmares. I wish we had met under much different circumstances. I wish that Gabriel, Connor, Madison, Lanika, and Brennen were all still alive today. But what I wish and what I want are not what happened. And out of these tragedies, out of these horrific losses, came a light. God made our paths cross, and I thank God for these tender mercies.

For if darkness, despair, hopelessness, and nothingness were all I felt and saw during these encounters, then that's all this nine-month saga would have been: a terribly sad, soul-crushing nightmare. But I saw more. I felt more. I felt compelled to bring these five grieving women together because I believed they could help one another. I sensed that Gabriel, Connor, Madison, Lanika, and Brennen could leave a legacy that would enlighten a blind world to the care needed (and which is sorely lacking) for young, grieving parents. I saw that Audra, Heather, Linda, Tania, and Allison each desired to bring solace to other parents hurting like they were. Out of the overwhelming grief into which all five of these mothers plunged, five hearts so generous emerged that they could not rest until they reached out to others also thrown into grief. These babies and their mothers are the angels for whom you may be searching.

And so, if your baby has died, this gathering of angels knows that you bear a grief so beyond definition that everything in your life must now be redefined. They know your spark for life has been extinguished, your hope for the future has been vanquished, and that your understanding of life has been shattered. They want to be compassionately available to you in your grief—they will not run from it, ignore it, or minimize it. By writing their heartfelt thoughts in this book, they choose to walk beside you in your grief. They want you to know you can make this journey, even though it may seem completely unbearable and interminable at times. They do not want you to feel alone. It is their hope that you will know your terrible pain is understood, and that you will feel comforted by reading the simple words of wisdom from five young mothers whose ties to their children are not in their terrible nightmares, but in their hopes of heaven.

Vicky has beautifully described how she came to know the five of us mothers. I believe this book would not be complete unless at least one of us described how we came to know her.

How did I come to know Vicky Leland? Looking back, it is hard to piece it all together because I met Vicky during the most tumultuous, tragic two weeks of my life. Recalling the event that brought Vicky into my life takes me back to my darkest days. But in them, I learned it is true: God really does bring you a beacon of hope and light when you need it most. Vicky was and still is my beacon of light.

I was introduced to Vicky first by the hospital volunteer chaplain who gave me a copy of Vicky's book titled, *The Work of Your Hand*. The chaplain told me this book was written and photographed by one of the staff nurses, and she thought I would find comfort in it. Well, that was the understatement of my life! Whenever I could find a quiet moment alone while Connor was in the hospital, usually while pumping, I would read Vicky's beautiful little book and wonder about its author. How could someone so perfectly understand the hopes and fears of NICU parents and then find such comforting words and images? After each chapter, I would go to the back of the book and study Vicky's photograph so that I could look for her in the NICU and maybe introduce myself. I would ask other nurses about her, only to learn she usually worked twice a week. I wondered if I would ever get the chance to meet her. One day I walked into the NICU and there was Vicky, assigned that day as Connor's nurse. I was overjoyed. I felt like we were really going to be taken care of. I felt like Connor could not be in safer hands. I thought it might even represent a turning point for Connor. What I have come to understand is that I would be taken care of and this was a turning point—not for Connor's survival, but for mine.

I felt an instant connection with Vicky like I've never experienced with any other person. Looking back now, I know that God put Vicky in my path for a purpose. As our bedside nurse with Connor, Vicky never seemed to tire of my endless questions. She answered them patiently, always being straightforward. She was honest, and I could tell then she wanted to offer me more hope. She wished things were different for us, but she also tenderly prepared us for what was to come. Strangely, I never felt angry with her like I had with some of the other doctors and nurses when she spoke the hard truths. When you're hearing so many horrible things you don't want to believe to be true, anger is one of the first reactions. I never once felt angry with Vicky.

When Vicky offered to take our pictures with Connor, I was overjoyed. We were so unprepared to deal with what was happening that the last thing we thought about was taking photographs. Those photos are now the only tangible way I have of remembering Connor. It brings me great peace knowing that as my memories of Connor fade, those pictures won't. I can go back to them whenever I need to.

I am trying to recall just how Vicky and I made the transition between her being Connor's nurse to her being my friend, advisor, motivator, confidant, and my inspiration. At the end of our first day together, Vicky gave me her contact information and said, "If you ever need me, give me a call." She told me later that this was not customary for her to do with her patients. I can only guess she must have been inspired by God to do that. Well, I needed her, and I called. I am so thankful that I did.

We had plenty of advisors during our last days with Connor. We had a wonderful staff of doctors and nurses who worked tirelessly to do everything possible to save Connor's life. We had our families by our side trying to help us make sense of the medical information. We had our church pastor and the hospital chaplain offering the word of God to us to help us through this most difficult time. Each of these advisors had their uniquely valid points of view: the medical information, the hopes and dreams of family, and the words of God. We needed someone to help us integrate these points of view in a manner that worked for us. Vicky was that person for us.

One of the first times I called Vicky was when we were faced with the decision to give Connor one more round of steroids, which could have had long-term negative effects for Connor if he lived. We wrestled with the decision, and Vicky was the one to help us finally find some clarity. She helped us know while the steroids held great risk and might not work, they were the last chance for Connor. She knew we would always need to believe, as Connor's parents, that he was given every chance for survival. She understood that, as a family and as Connor's parents, we were not ready to lose him. Can you imagine starting a friendship in this way, by literally facing life and death together? Twenty-four hours after that last round of steroids, I called Vicky again. It was around midnight, and I needed her. I needed her to come to the hospital to be with us as Connor died. She had offered, and we wanted her to take photos of us with Connor one last time—the only time we ever held our son. In the middle of the night, she came without hesitation. Vicky was with us as we loved Connor into heaven. Two weeks earlier, she had been a complete stranger to us, but that night, as our beloved son died in our arms, it was perfectly right and normal for Vicky to be there with us.

After Connor's death, I was truly walking in the valley of the shadow of death, and Vicky walked with me. Only a few special souls can or want to understand what this grief is like. Many may think they want to know, but after getting a small dose of the intense feelings of confusion, anger, depression, and sadness, I have found most run the other way. Vicky is that one special soul who chose to walk beside me and beside the other mothers writing this book. She formed loving bonds with each of us while we faced the deaths of our dearly loved babies. She didn't try to change our grief, invalidate it, or minimize it. She just listened to it, tried to help us make sense of it, and is now turning it into something that will honor our children and help others who will go through this type of grief.

I believe Vicky is our angel walking this earth. Words cannot describe how thankful I am that God put Vicky in my life, and that she was willing to walk with me, and all of us, through the dark valley of the shadow of death and towards hope.

A Special Thanks
to the March of Dimes

*T*he March of Dimes is mentioned in this book on several occasions. This non-profit organization has been a frequent thread, weaving in and out of the Good Grief Group's journey together. It was a March of Dimes project on which Vicky was volunteering that first brought the group together. It was often the March of Dimes that offered the Good Grief mothers meaningful volunteer opportunities to honor the memories of their babies (lobbying legislators on behalf of babies and pregnant women, speaking on parent panels at hospitals to teach NICU staff how to care for grieving families, fundraising for research to prevent prematurity, etc.) The Texas Chapter of the March of Dimes so valued the promise of this book to help families experiencing the loss of a baby that they awarded our group a small grant to help us with the initial costs of writing this book. And midway through the writing of this book, Vicky made a career change from bedside NICU nursing at a hospital to become the West Regional Director of NICU Family Support for the March of Dimes.

The mission of the March of Dimes is to improve the health of babies by preventing birth defects, premature birth, and infant mortality. As five families who experienced the death of their babies due to premature births, and as a nurse who witnessed for twenty years the heartbreaking devastation that birth defects and prematurity cause, we wish to extend our appreciation to the March of Dimes. Your mission is very dear to our hearts. We thank you for your tireless efforts in ensuring a healthy start in life for every baby. Congratulations on the many successes you have been involved in over the years—the development of a regionalized system of NICUs throughout our country, the development of PKU testing, the development of surfactant therapy for premature baby lungs, the fortification of grain products with folic acid to help reduce neural tube birth defects, and the development of nitric oxide therapy. You have our sincere gratitude for all your work. We know many miracle babies have survived their premature beginnings because of the research you have funded and because of the educational and advocacy efforts you have spearheaded. But we also know—all too well—that babies continue to die every day. We thank you as you continue to strive to save future babies the same fate our babies suffered.

About the Authors

Victoria Leland, RN, earned her Bachelor of Science Degree in Nursing from the University of the Incarnate Word in San Antonio, Texas. She practiced as a hospital bedside nurse for twenty-seven years, twenty of which were in Neonatal Intensive Care. She is an accomplished photographer and has completed two national traveling photo exhibits for the March of Dimes. She is the mother of a prematurely born child and also the author of *The Work of Your Hand: Christian Meditations for Parents of Critically Ill Babies in Neonatal Intensive Care.*

Linda Bailey, an accountant by profession, found her life turned upside down very unexpectedly when her twins arrived sixteen weeks prematurely. Madison lived two days, and Kaitlyn survived a difficult four-month journey in the NICU. Linda experienced a complicated form of grief as she rejoiced in the miraculous survival of one daughter, while profoundly grieving the loss of her beloved second daughter. Linda's search for healing led her to a group of other grieving mothers and her NICU nurse, with whom she journaled and became extremely active in community volunteerism.

Allison Guild, a middle school Special Education teacher by profession, was a first-time mother when her son Brennen was born. He arrived twelve weeks prematurely and passed away in the NICU at nine days of age. Left with a broken heart, Allison's search for healing led her to a group of other grieving mothers gathered together by her NICU nurse, with whom she journaled (using her love of analogies to write about her grief) and became involved in community volunteerism projects that honored Brennen's life.

Tania Hossain, a telecommunications customer service rep, is a native of Bangladesh. Her third daughter, Lanika, was born three months early and spent several months in a NICU before she succumbed to complications of prematurity and died. In the wake of

Lanika's death, Tania, her husband, and two elementary aged daughters struggled immensely with their shattered family dreams and profound grief. Tania's search for healing found real solace in the welcoming friendships of other grieving mothers and their NICU nurse, with whom she met regularly and journaled. In her lovely English-as-a-second-language way, Tania found expression for her sorrow and true strength for her grief journey.

Heather Gray, a highly successful software engineer, was a first time mother when her son Connor was born. He arrived sixteen weeks prematurely and passed away at twenty days of age. Leaving the NICU without Connor left Heather's world and dreams shattered. After much searching, she found solace for her grief most effectively when she journaled, forged friendships, and did community service projects with her NICU nurse and other grieving NICU mothers.

Audra Fox-Murphy was a young bank teller and newly married military wife when her son Gabriel was born. All her lovely dreams of building a family came crashing down when her son arrived fifteen weeks early. When Gabriel died at sixty-seven days of age, Audra was left devastated. Her search for healing led her to a group of other NICU moms who were grieving the loss of their babies. She found great comfort as they shared structured journaling, deep discussions, tears, laughter, and time together doing meaningful community service projects that honored the memories of their beloved babies.